HAL•LEONARD®
GUITAR PLAY-ALONG

AUDIO
ACCESS
INCLUDED

PLAYBACK+
Speed • Pitch • Balance • Loop

STEVE VAI

T0070698

To access audio visit:
www.halleonard.com/mylibrary

Enter Code
7524-7212-6599-9061

Cover photo © PAIGE K. PARSONS / ATLASICONS.COM

ISBN 978-1-4950-5768-7

Visit Hal Leonard Online at
www.halleonard.com

Contact us:
Hal Leonard
7777 West Bluemound Road
Milwaukee, WI 53213
Email: info@halleonard.com

In Europe, contact:
Hal Leonard Europe Limited
42 Wigmore Street
Marylebone, London, W1U 2RN
Email: info@halleonardeurope.com

In Australia, contact:
Hal Leonard Australia Pty. Ltd.
4 Lentara Court
Cheltenham, Victoria, 3192 Australia
Email: info@halleonard.com.au

Guitar Notation Legend

THE MUSICAL STAFF shows pitches and rhythms and is divided by bar lines into measures. Pitches are named after the first seven letters of the alphabet.

TABLATURE graphically represents the guitar fingerboard. Each horizontal line represents a string, and each number represents a fret.

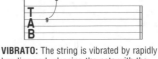
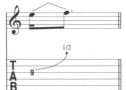

Notes:

Strings:
high E
B
G
D
A
low E

4th string, 2nd fret

1st & 2nd strings open, played together

open D chord

HALF-STEP BEND: Strike the note and bend up 1/2 step.

WHOLE-STEP BEND: Strike the note and bend up one step.

GRACE NOTE BEND: Strike the note and immediately bend up as indicated.

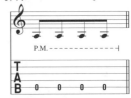

SLIGHT (MICROTONE) BEND: Strike the note and bend up 1/4 step.

BEND AND RELEASE: Strike the note and bend up as indicated, then release back to the original note. Only the first note is struck.

PRE-BEND: Bend the note as indicated, then strike it.

VIBRATO: The string is vibrated by rapidly bending and releasing the note with the fretting hand.

PALM MUTING: The note is partially muted by the pick hand lightly touching the string(s) just before the bridge.

HAMMER-ON: Strike the first (lower) note with one finger, then sound the higher note (on the same string) with another finger by fretting it without picking.

PULL-OFF: Place both fingers on the notes to be sounded. Strike the first note and without picking, pull the finger off to sound the second (lower) note.

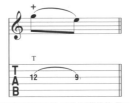

LEGATO SLIDE: Strike the first note and then slide the same fret-hand finger up or down to the second note. The second note is not struck.

SHIFT SLIDE: Same as legato slide, except the second note is struck.

TRILL: Very rapidly alternate between the notes indicated by continuously hammering on and pulling off.

TAPPING: Hammer ("tap") the fret indicated with the pick-hand index or middle finger and pull off to the note fretted by the fret hand.

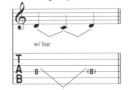

NATURAL HARMONIC: Strike the note while the fret-hand lightly touches the string directly over the fret indicated.

PINCH HARMONIC: The note is fretted normally and a harmonic is produced by adding the edge of the thumb or the tip of the index finger of the pick hand to the normal pick attack.

TREMOLO PICKING: The note is picked as rapidly and continuously as possible.

VIBRATO BAR DIVE AND RETURN: The pitch of the note or chord is dropped a specified number of steps (in rhythm), then returned to the original pitch.

VIBRATO BAR SCOOP: Depress the bar just before striking the note, then quickly release the bar.

VIBRATO BAR DIP: Strike the note and then immediately drop a specified number of steps, then release back to the original pitch.

Additional Musical Definitions

(accent) • Accentuate note (play it louder).

(staccato) • Play the note short.

D.S. al Coda • Go back to the sign (%), then play until the measure marked "*To Coda*," then skip to the section labelled "**Coda**."

D.C. al Fine • Go back to the beginning of the song and play until the measure marked "*Fine*" (end).

Fill • Label used to identify a brief melodic figure which is to be inserted into the arrangement.

N.C. • Harmony is implied.

 • Repeat measures between signs.

 • When a repeated section has different endings, play the first ending only the first time and the second ending only the second time.

CONTENTS

The Attitude Song

By Steve Vai

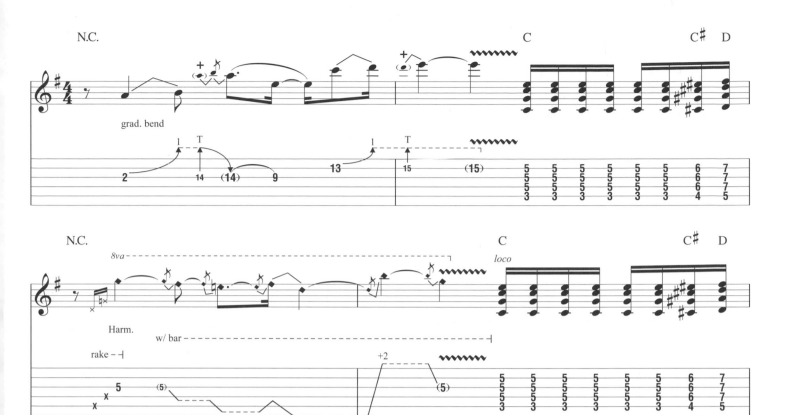

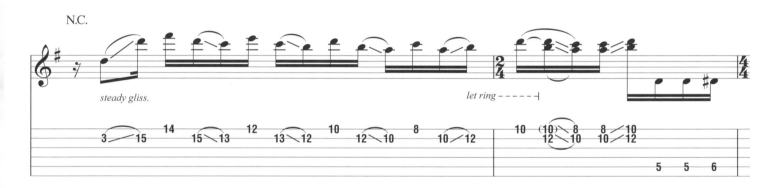

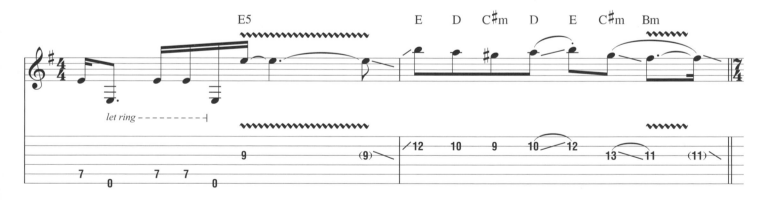

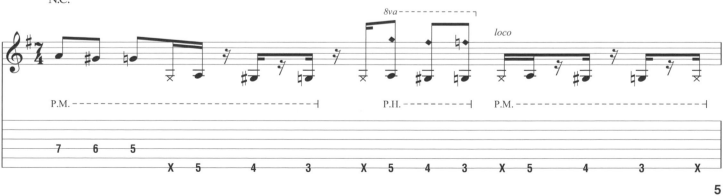

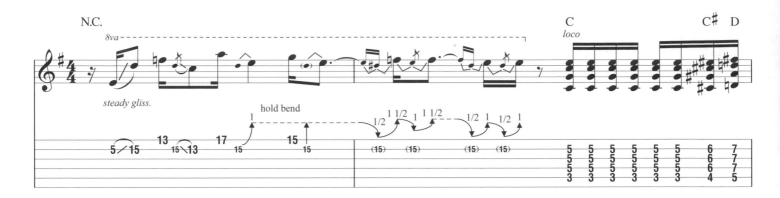

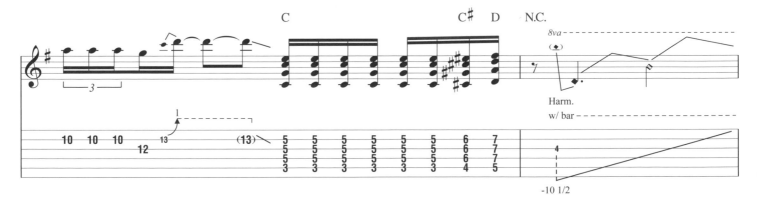

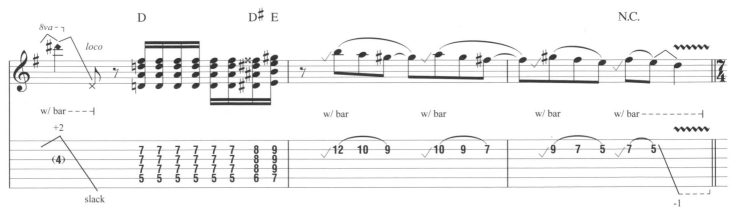

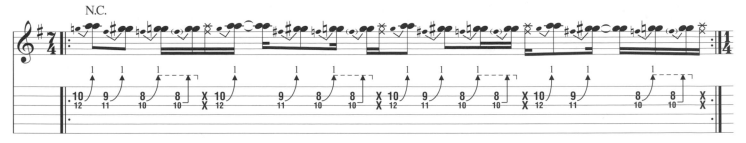

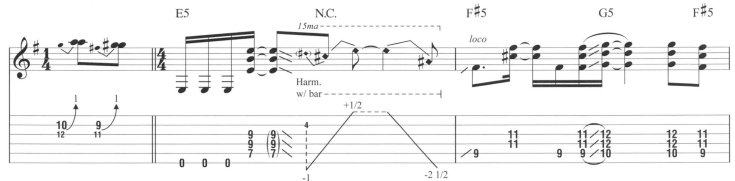

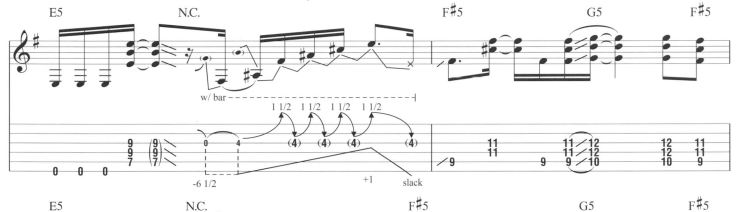

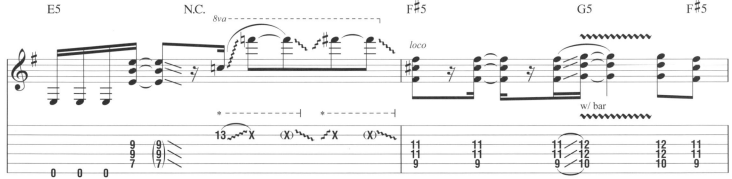

*Grab string w/ fingernail at 13th fret and pull downward over fretboard edge, then release.

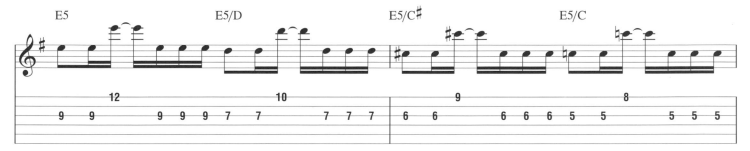

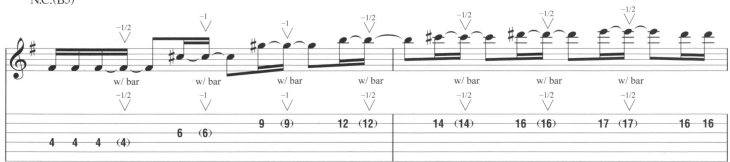

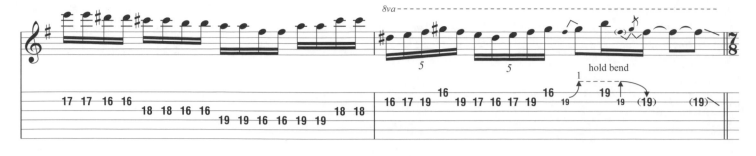

N.C.

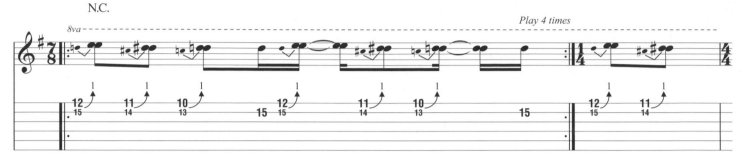

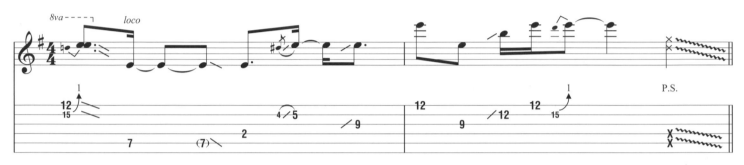

N.C.

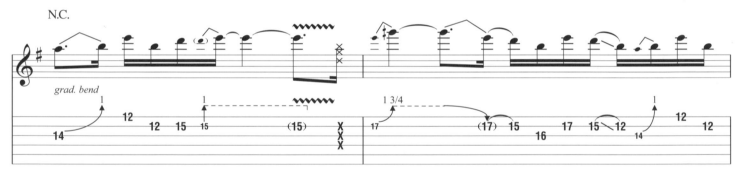

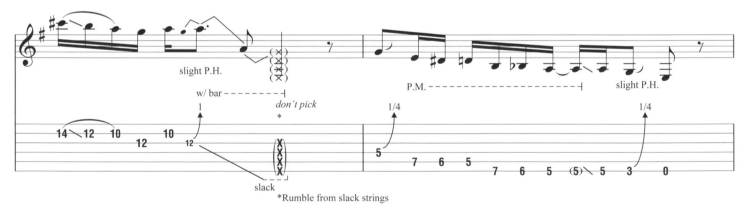

*Rumble from slack strings

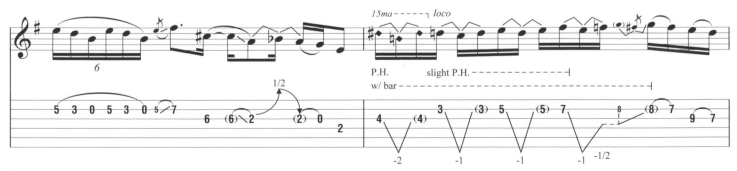

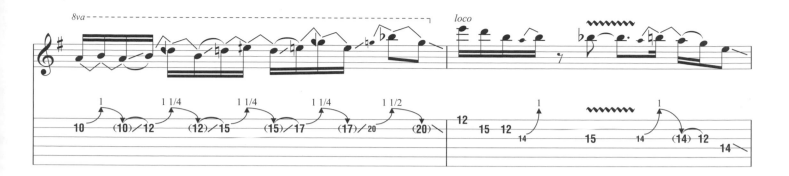

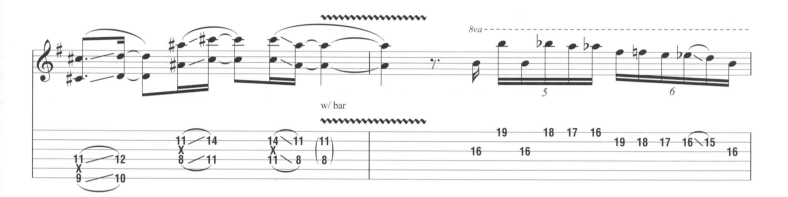

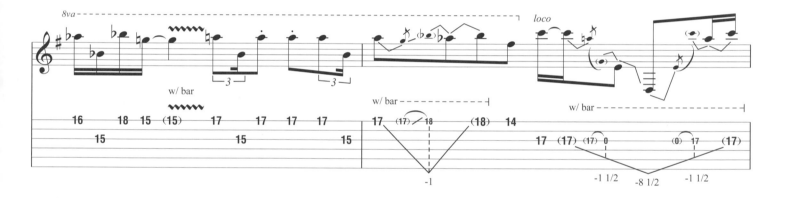

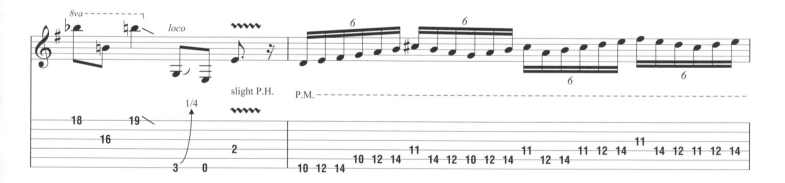

9

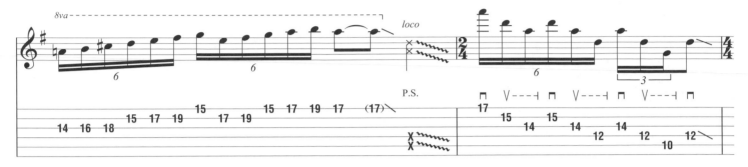

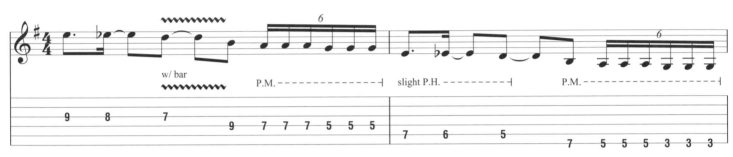

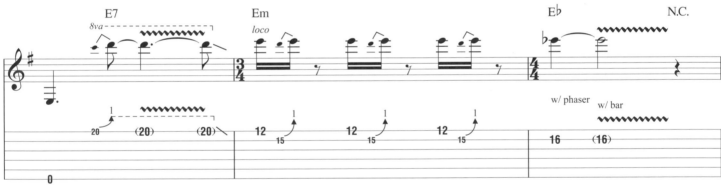

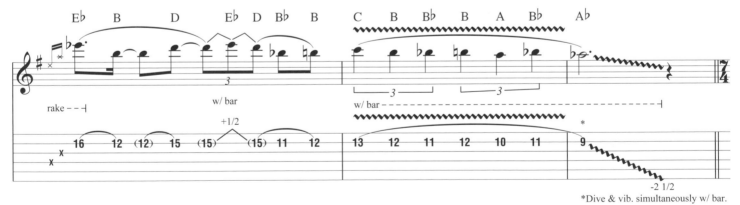

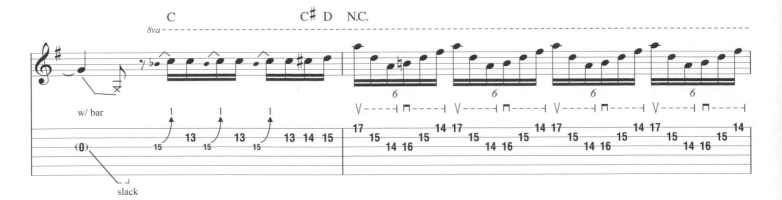

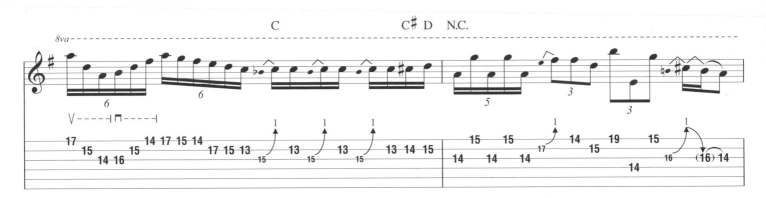

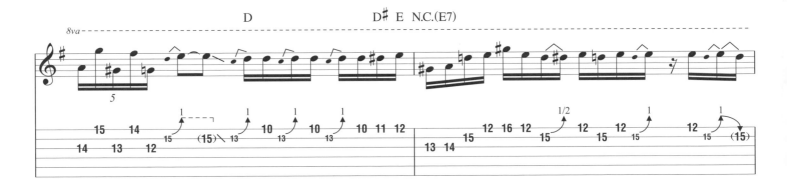

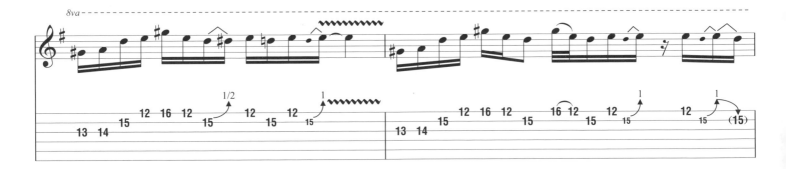

The Crying Machine

By Steve Vai

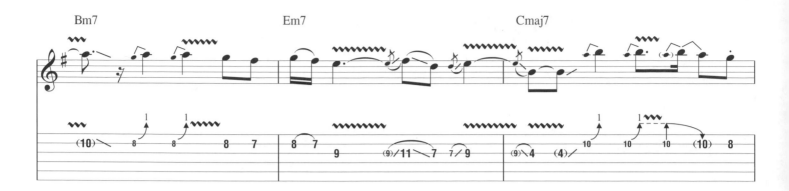

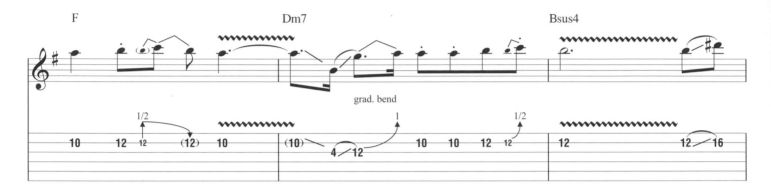

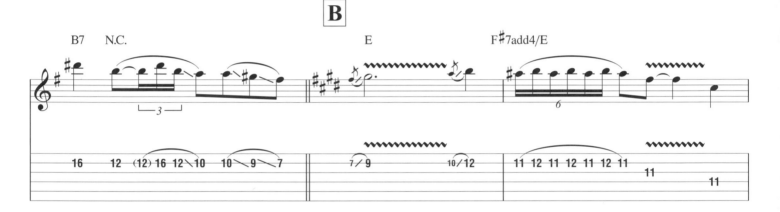

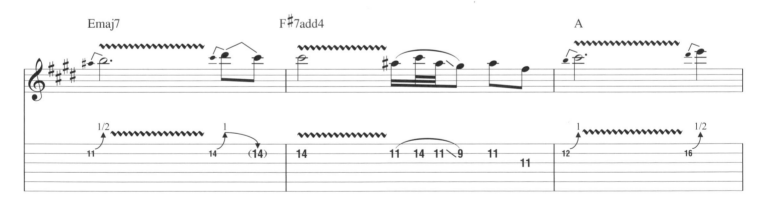

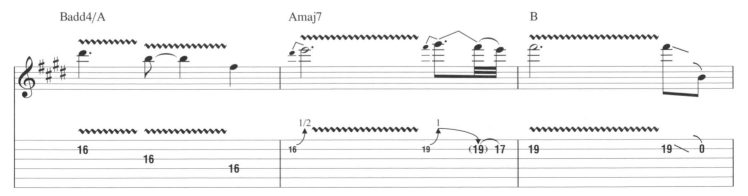

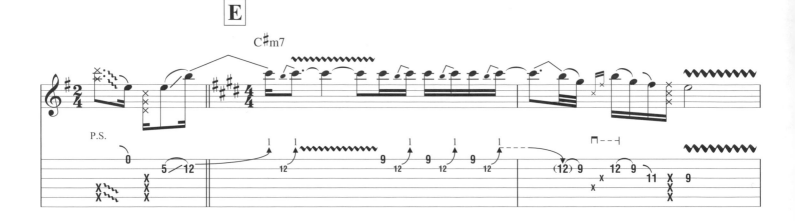

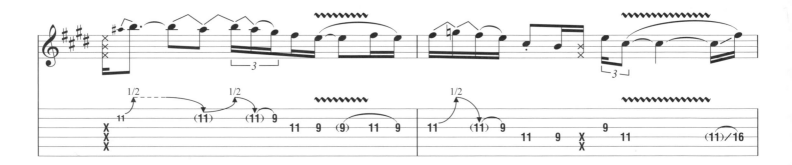

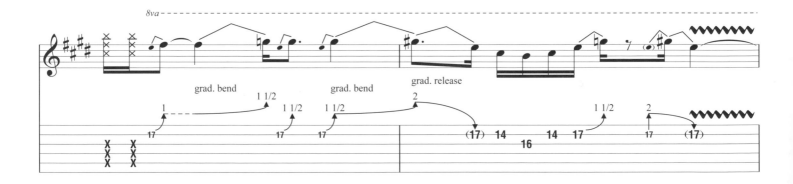

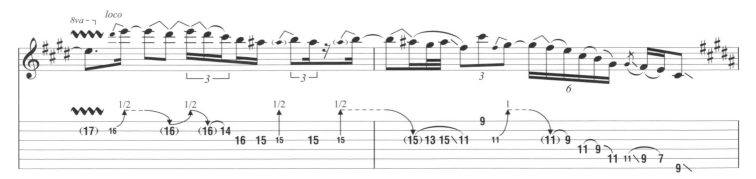

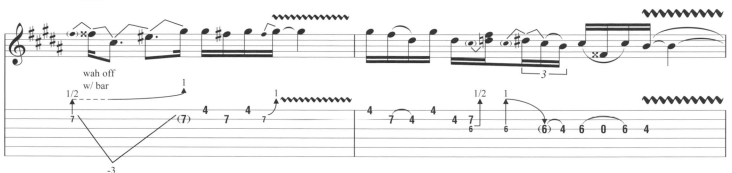

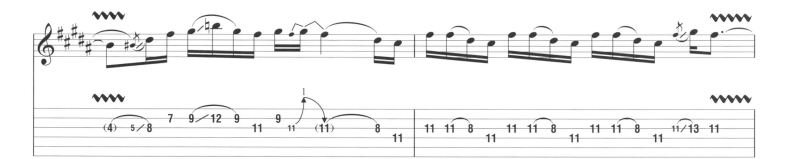

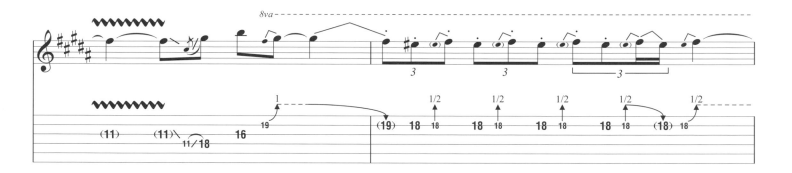

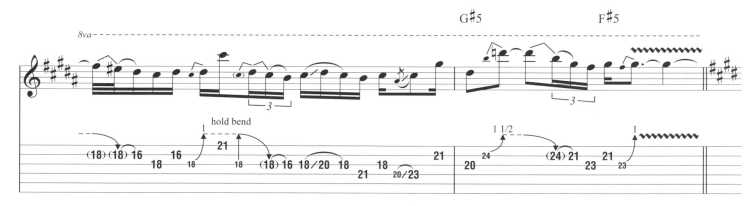

F

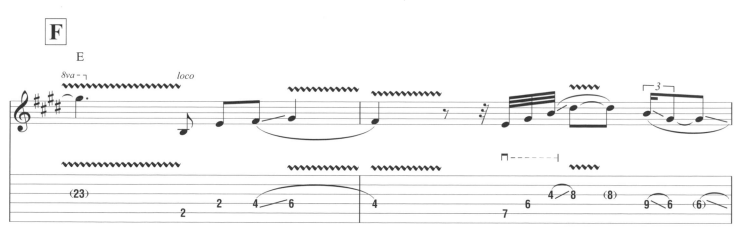

F#7add4/E

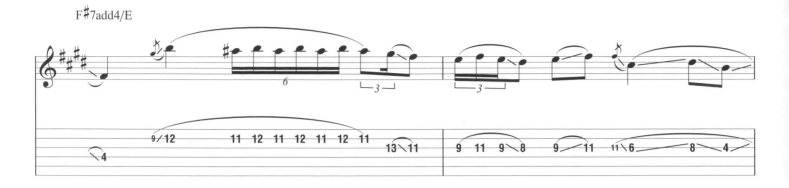

Emaj7

F#7add4

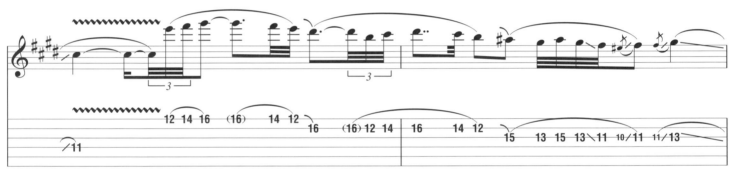

A

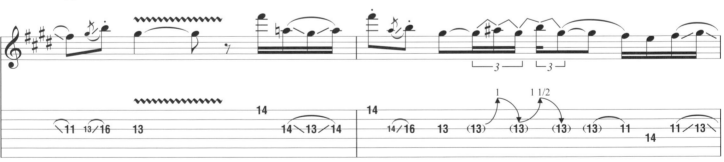

B/A

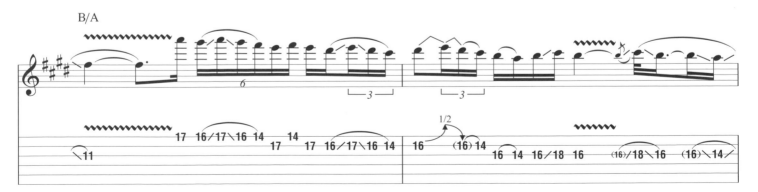

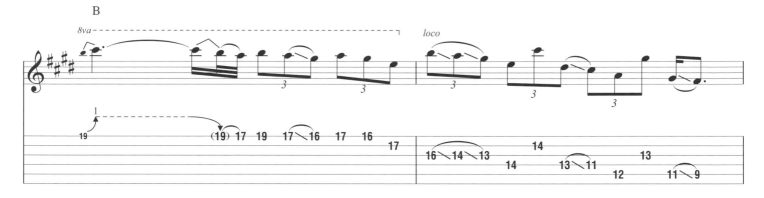

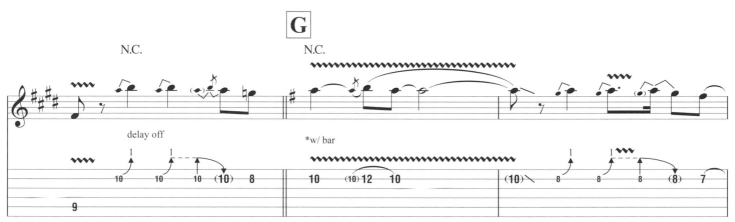

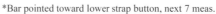

*Bar pointed toward lower strap button, next 7 meas.

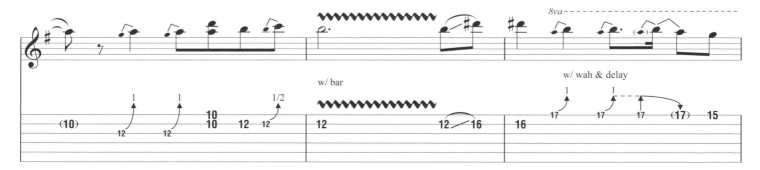

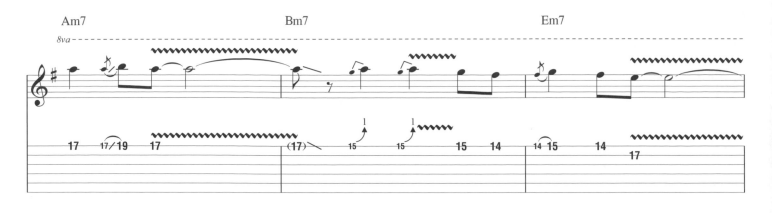

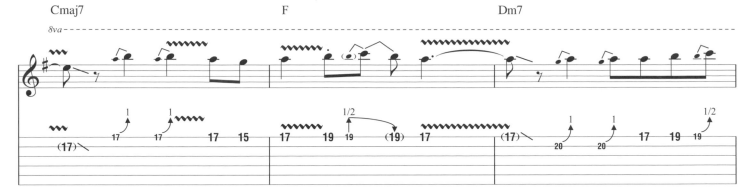

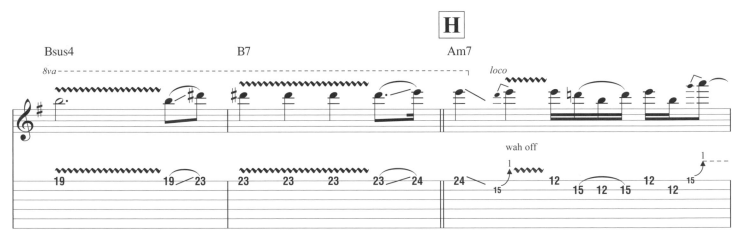

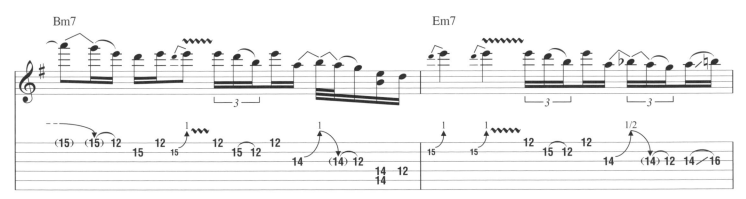

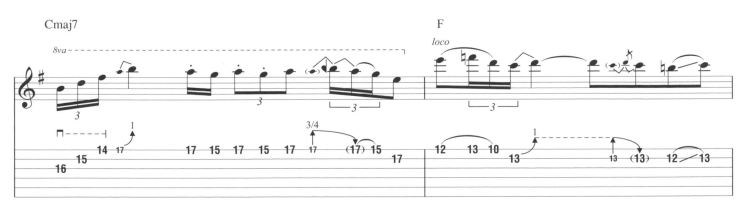

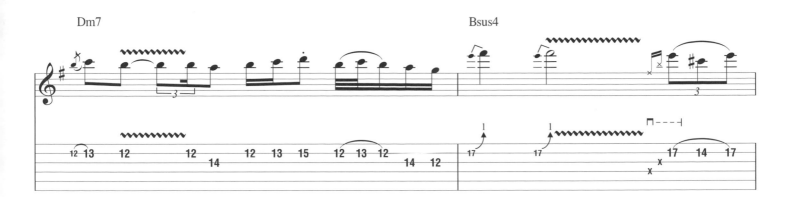

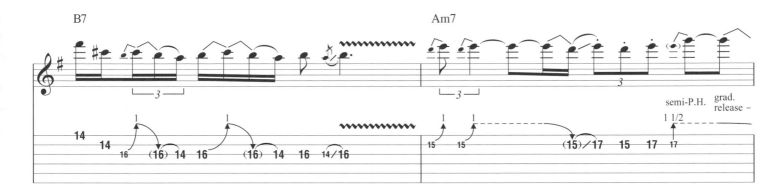

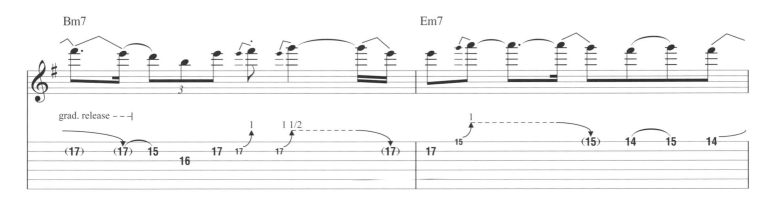

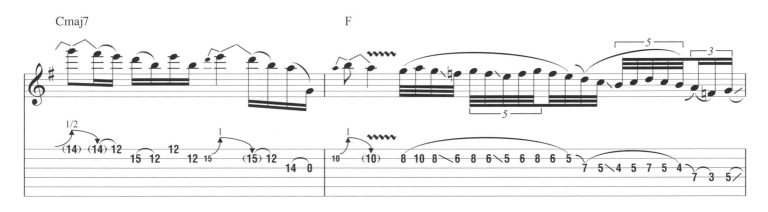

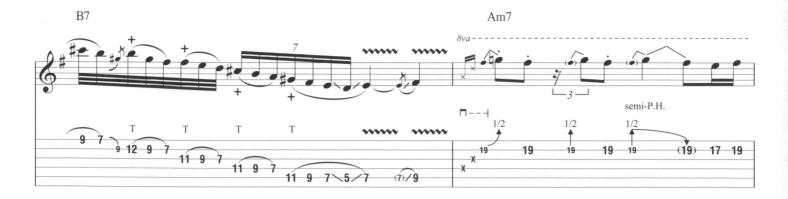

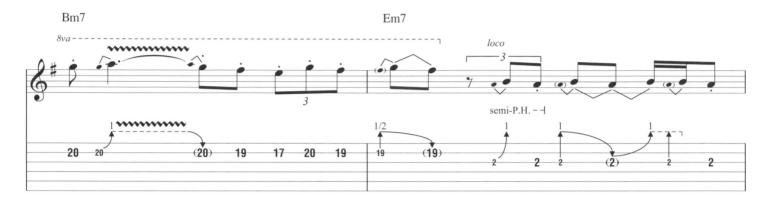

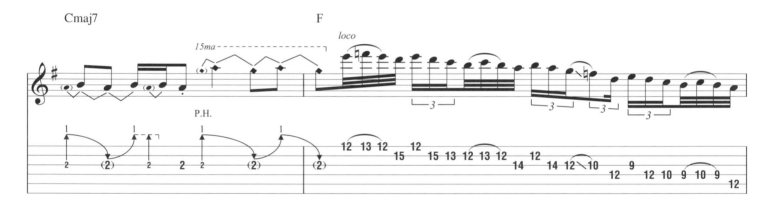

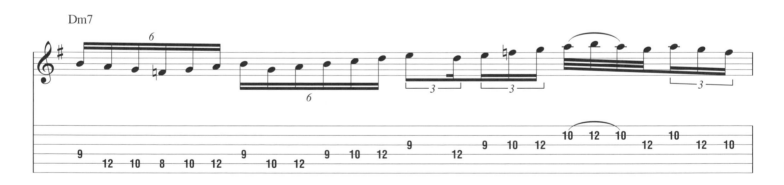

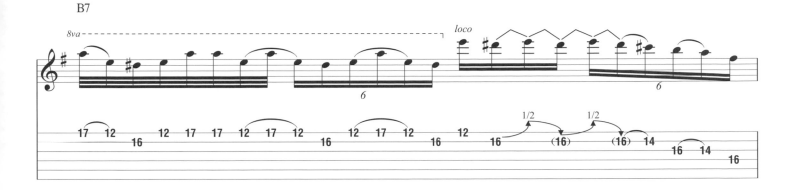

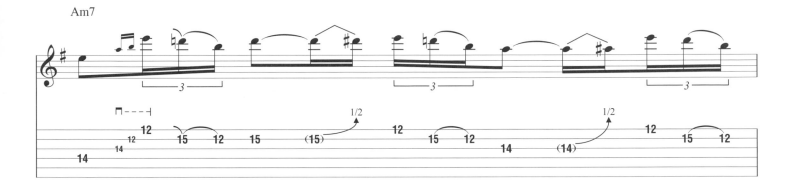

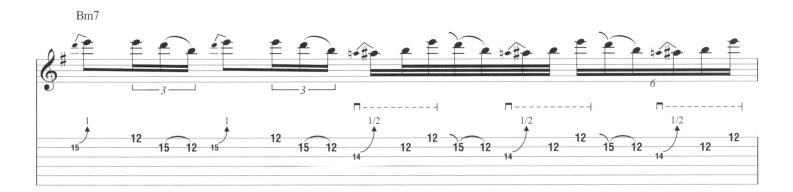

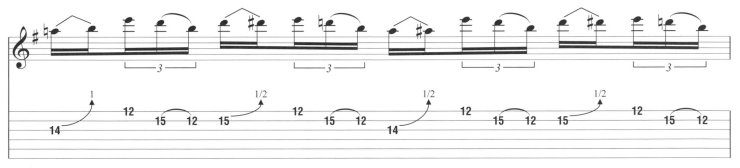

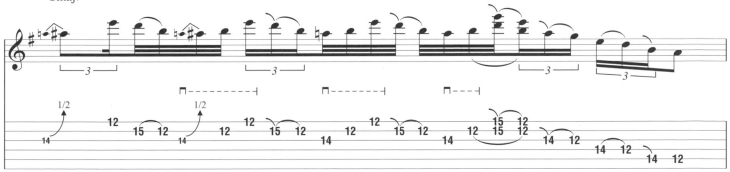

F   Dm7

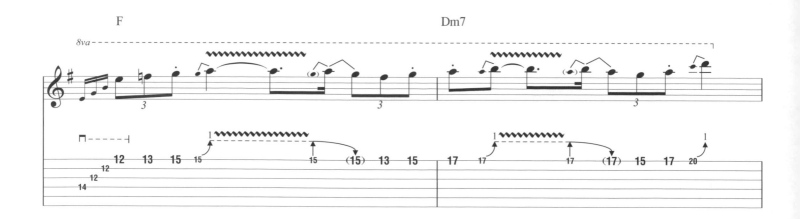

Bsus4   B7

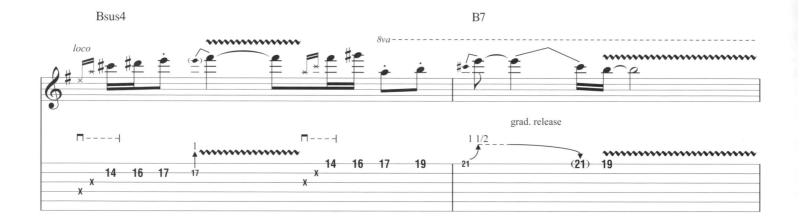

Begin fade

Am7

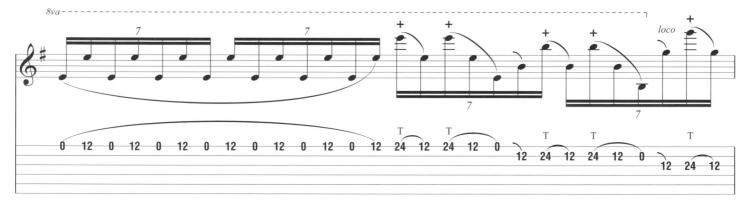

Bm7

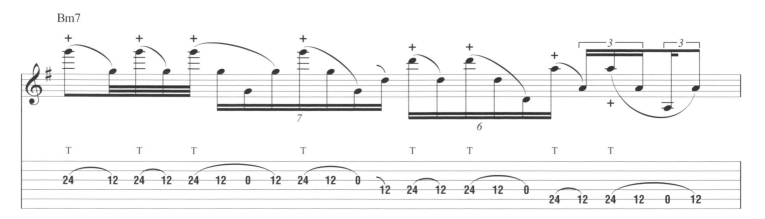

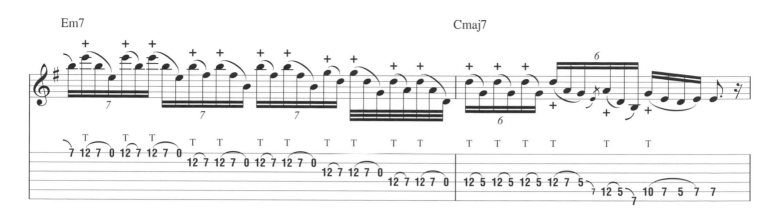

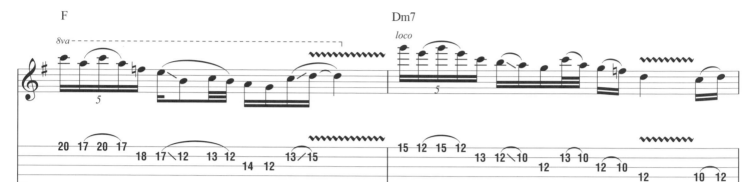

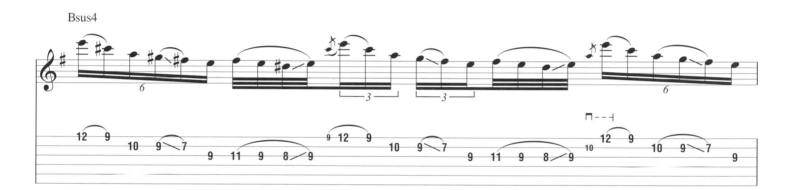

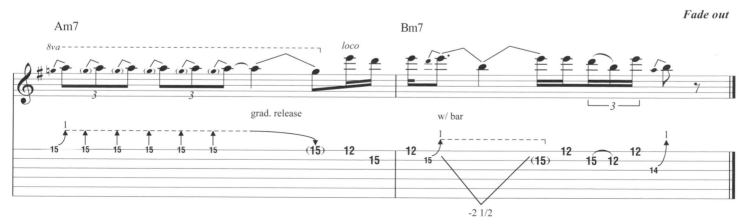

Die to Live

By Steve Vai

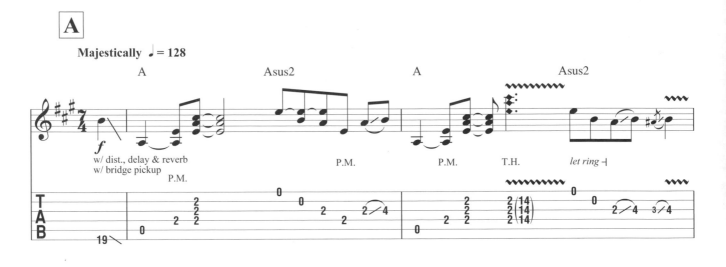

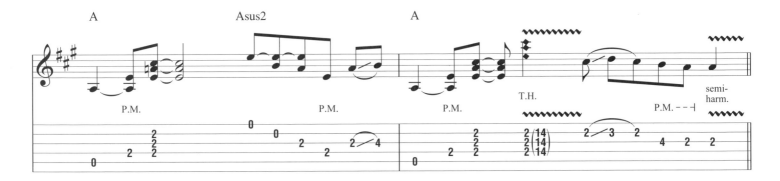

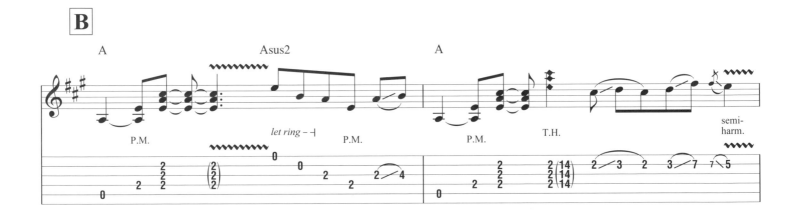

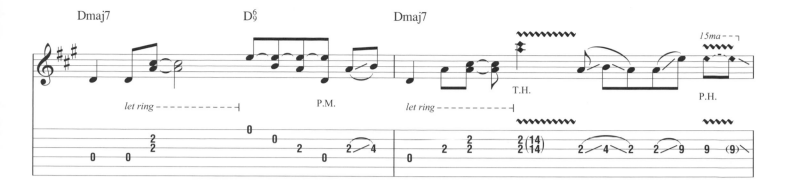

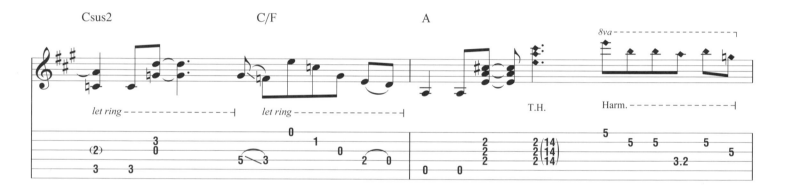

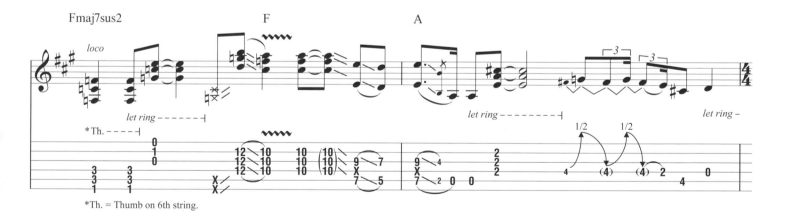

*Th. = Thumb on 6th string.

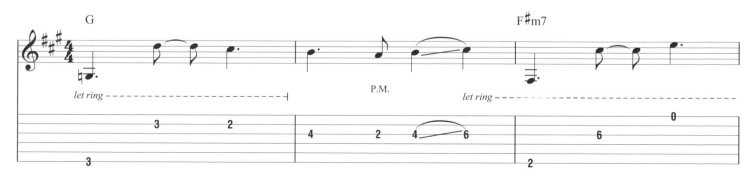

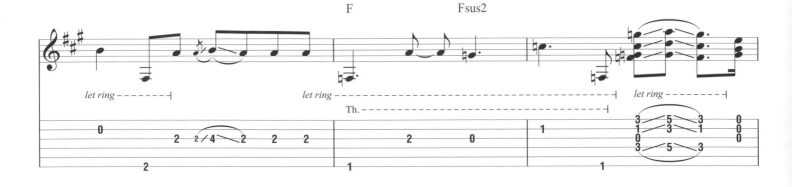

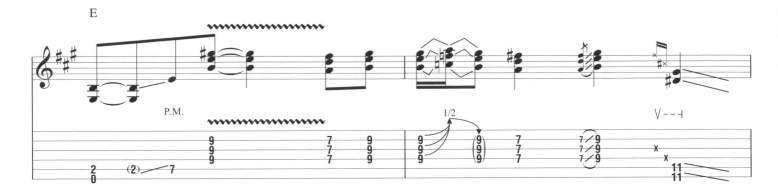

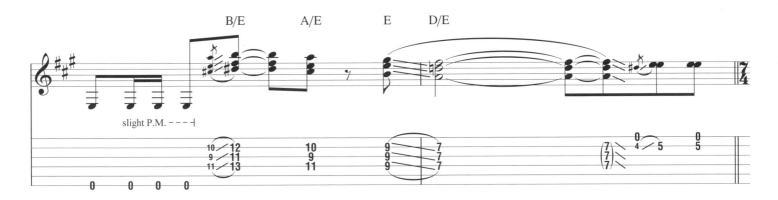

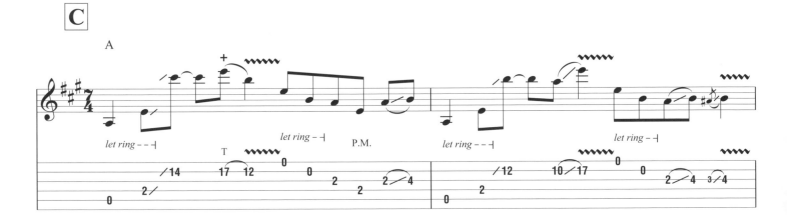

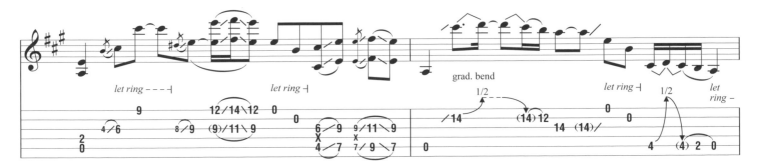

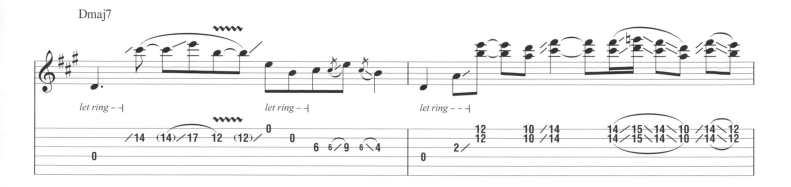

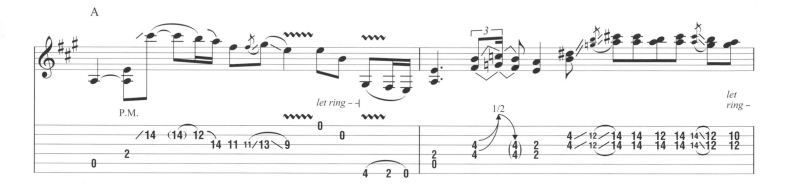

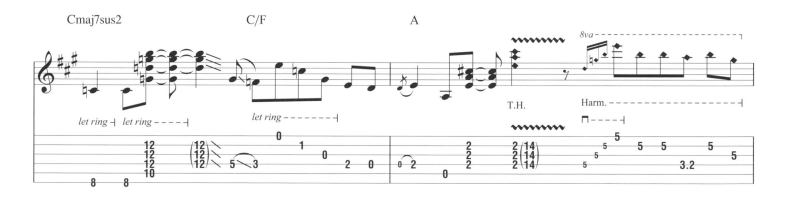

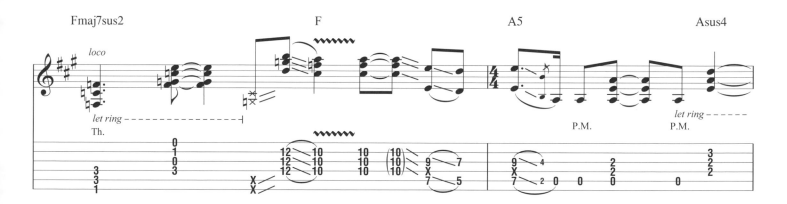

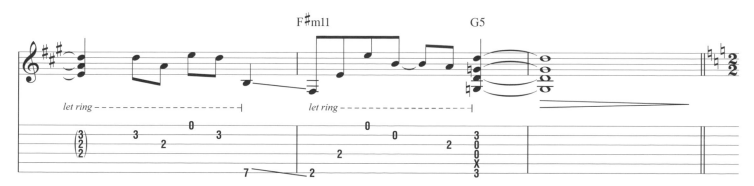

D

F/B♭   Am(add9)

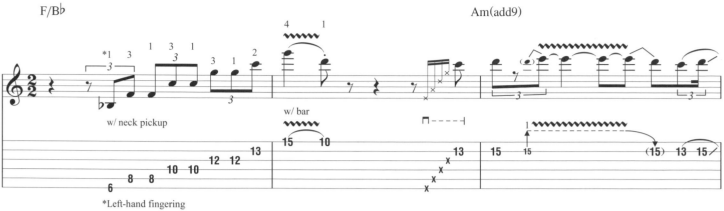

w/ neck pickup

*Left-hand fingering

E♭/A♭

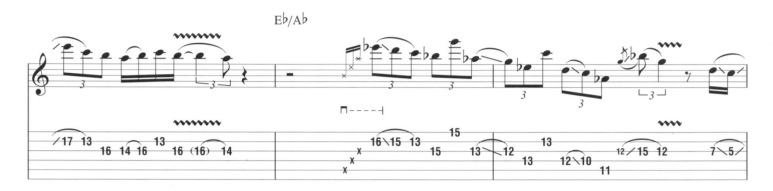

Gm(add9)   C#7♭5

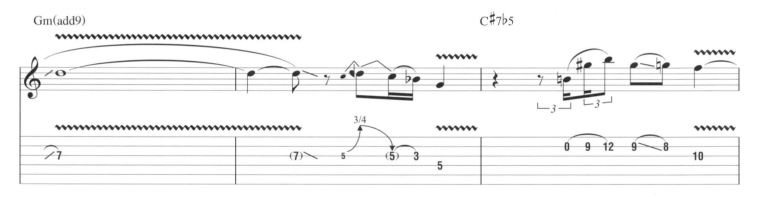

C/D

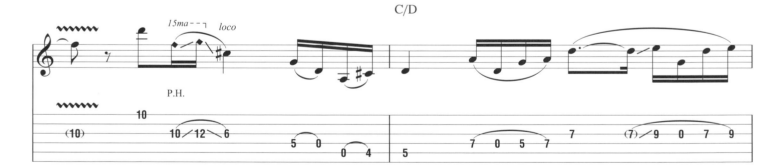

D#+7

30

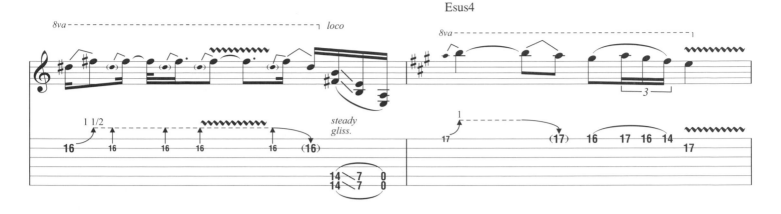

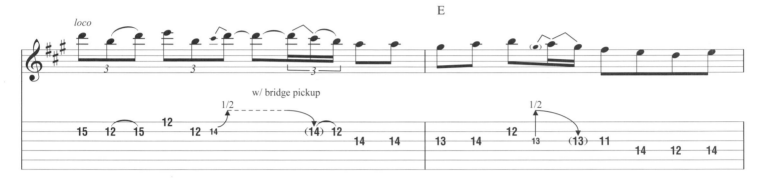

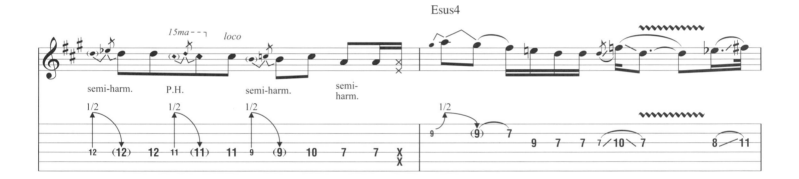

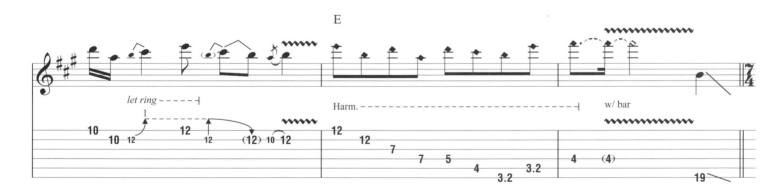

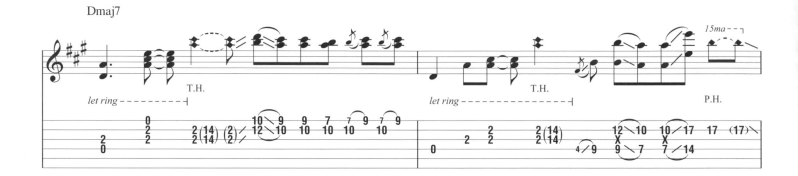

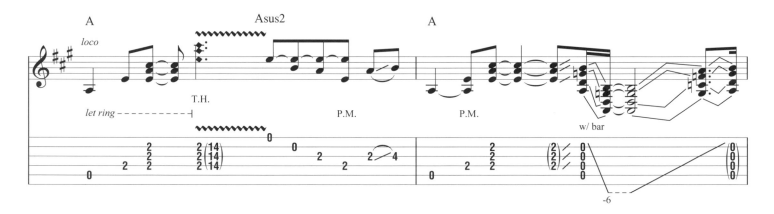

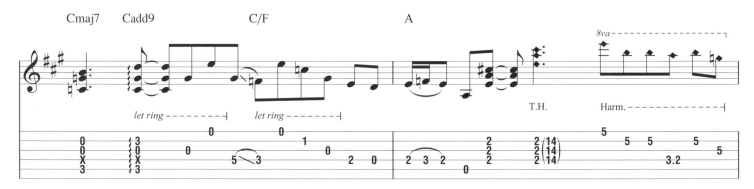

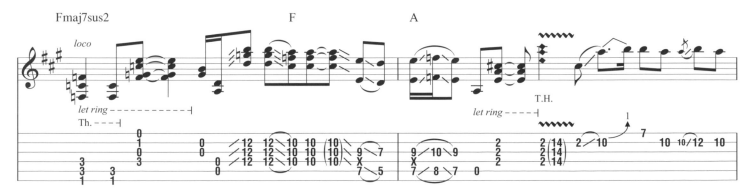

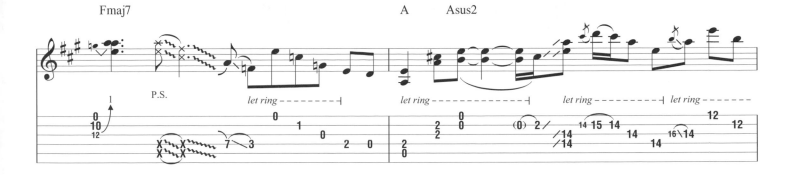

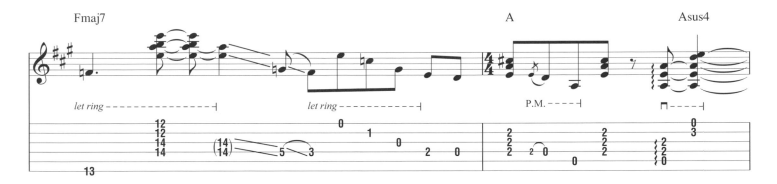

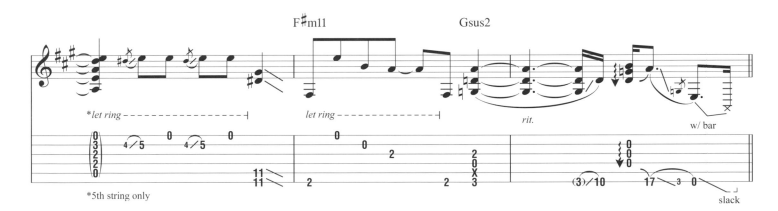

F

Free time

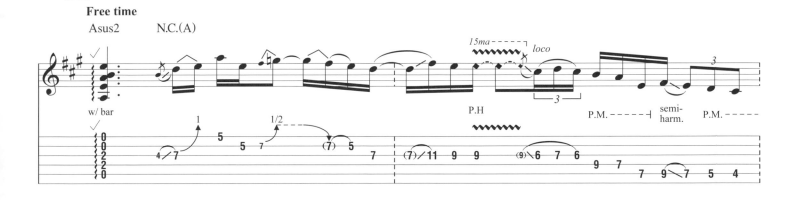

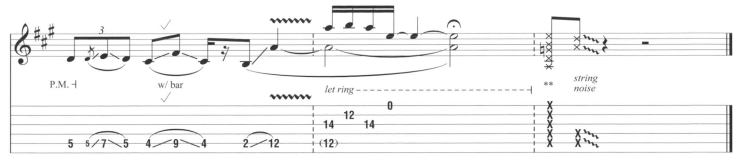

**Place R.H. on strings.

For the Love of God

By Steve Vai

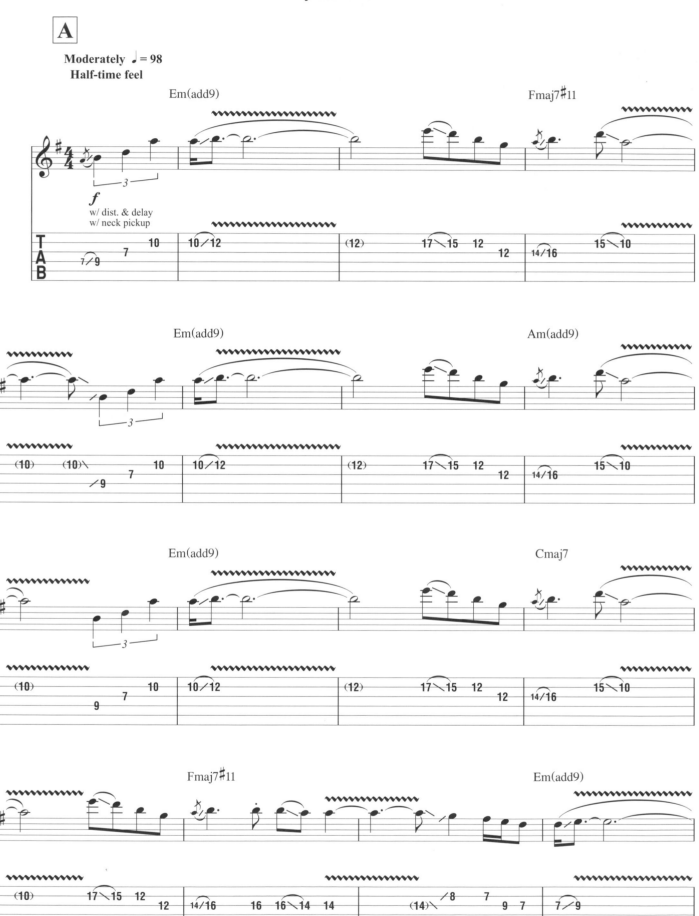

B

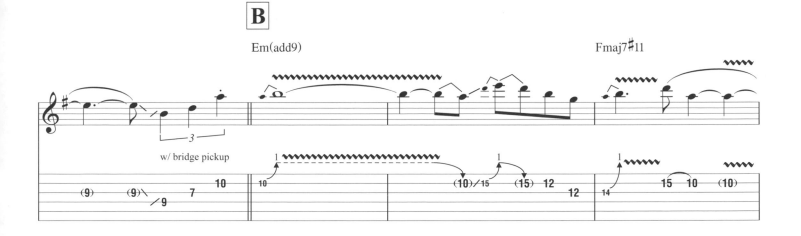

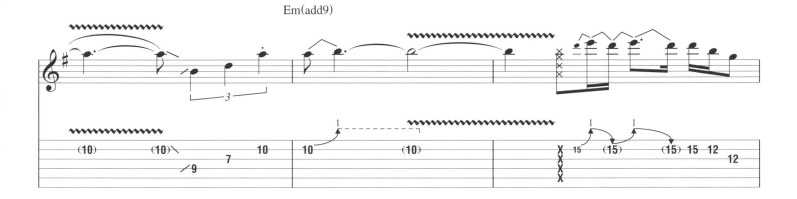

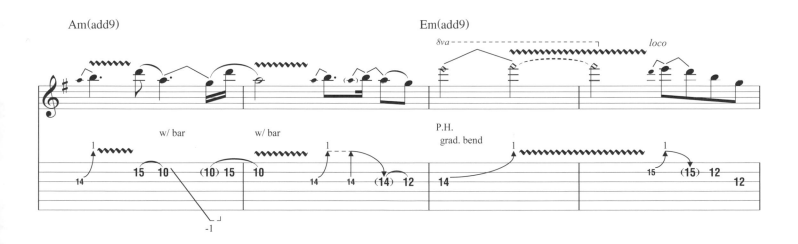

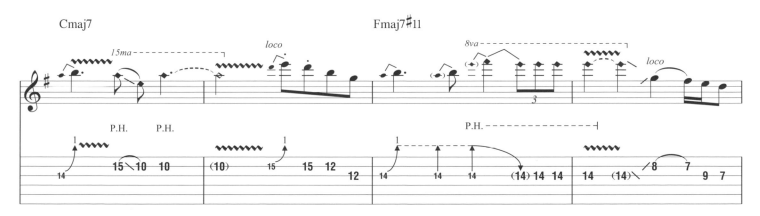

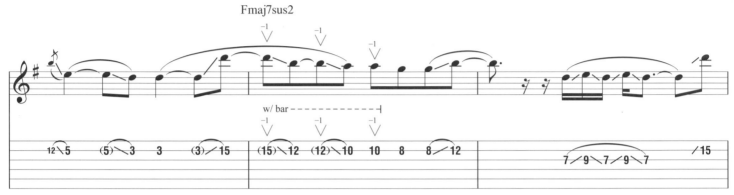

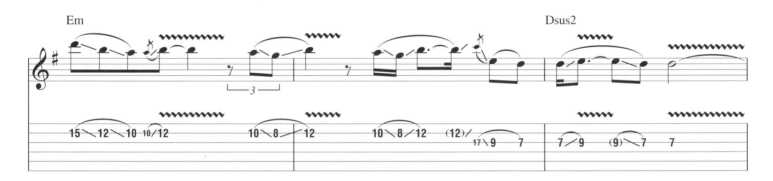

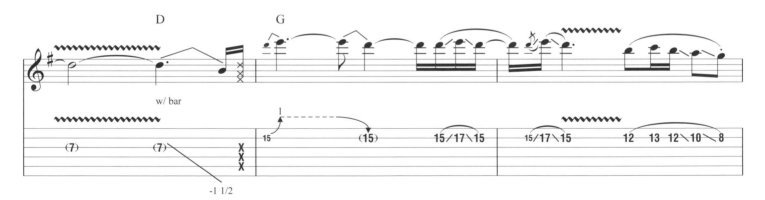

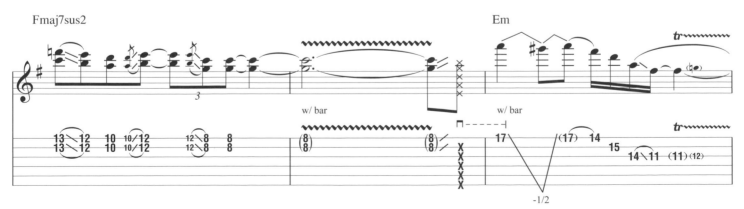

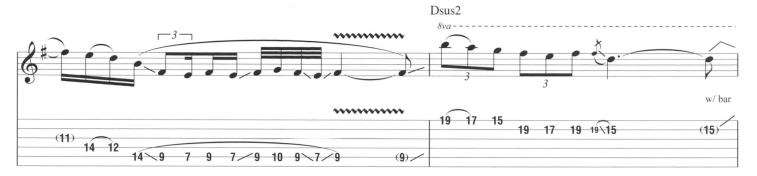

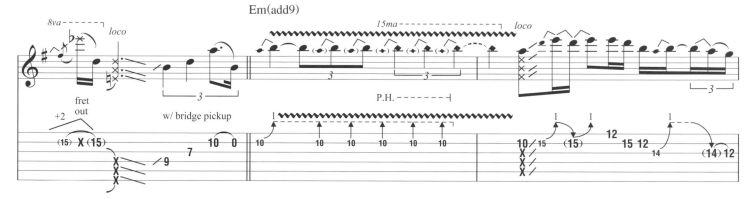

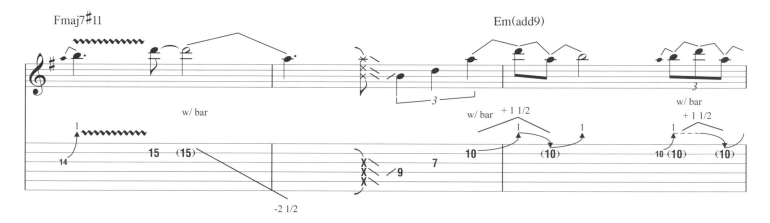

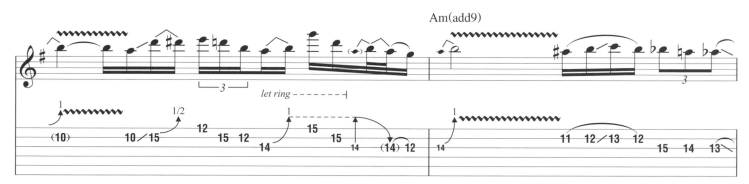

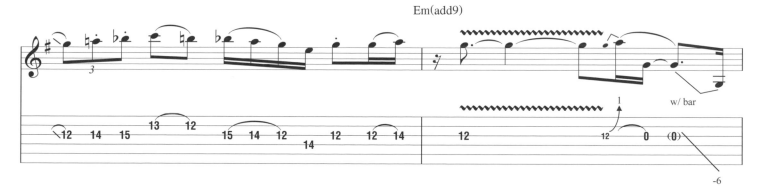

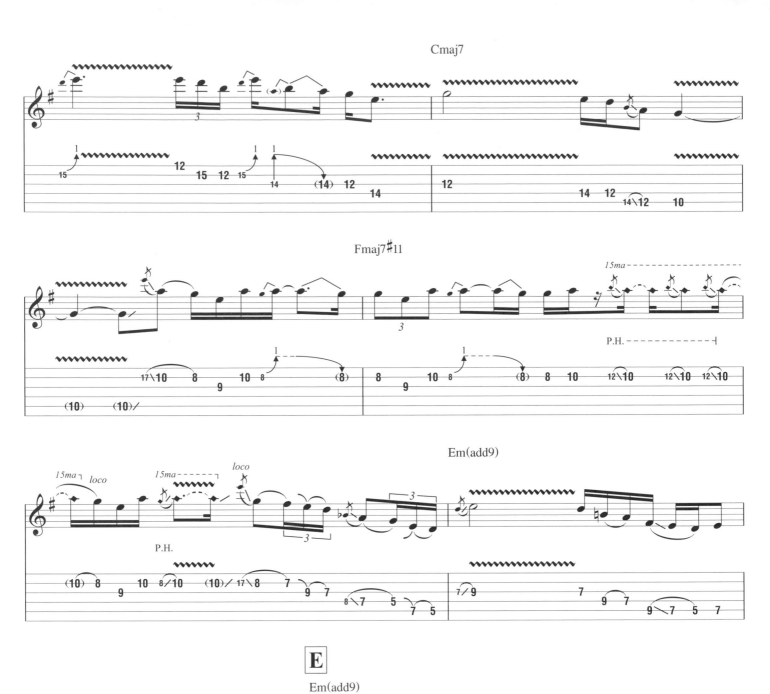

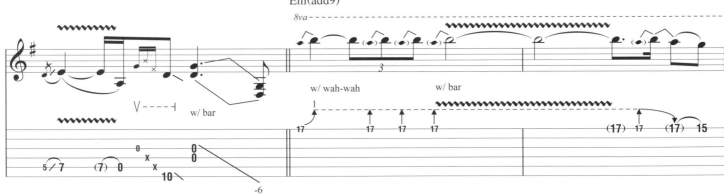

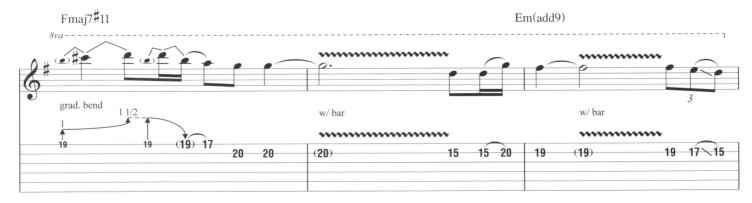

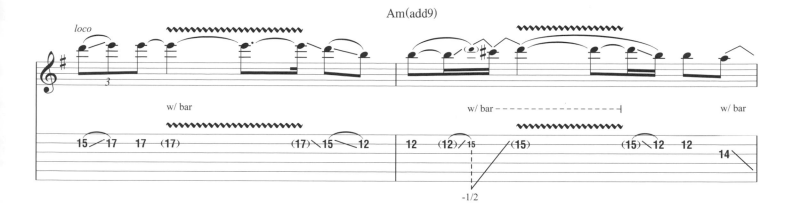

Am(add9)

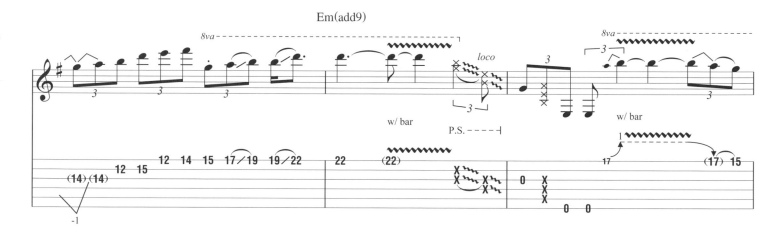

Em(add9)

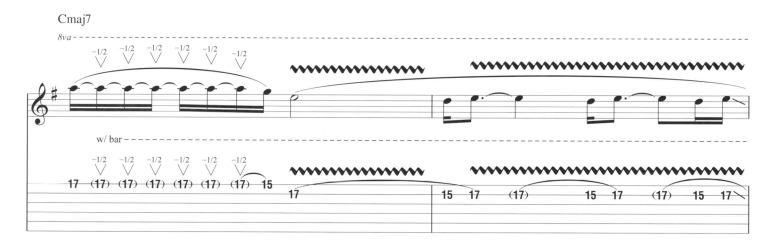

Cmaj7

Fmaj7♯11

*Depress & release bar quickly w/ edge of hand, causing slight flutter on return.

**Open strings sound sympathetically from bar use.

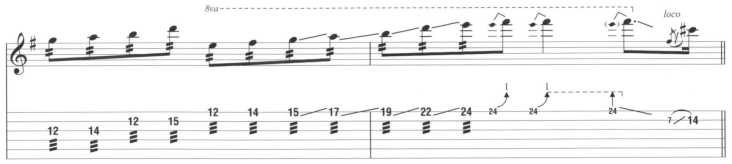

F

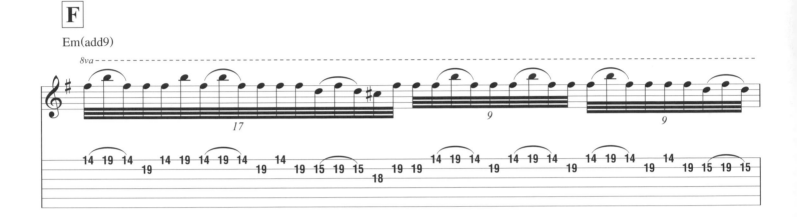

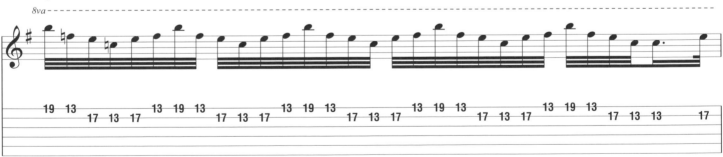

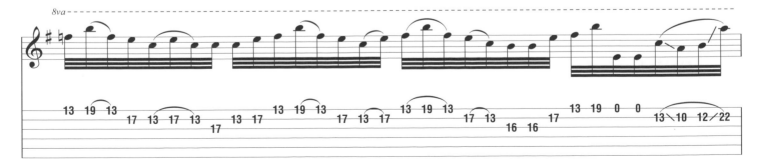

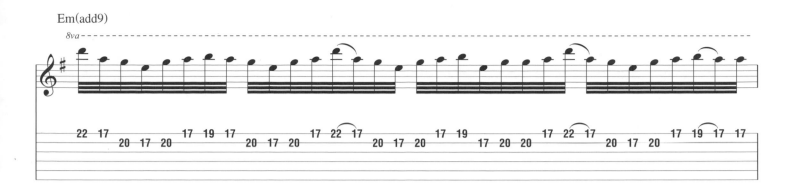

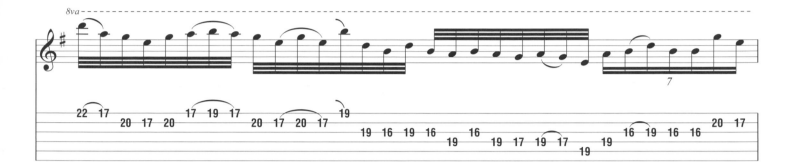

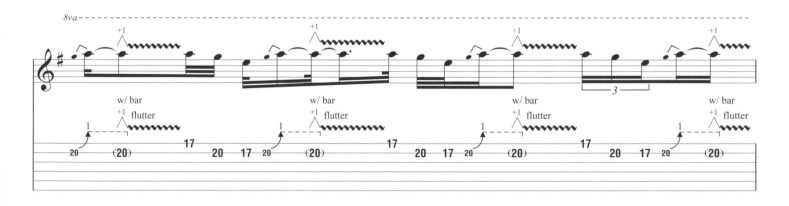

Cmaj7

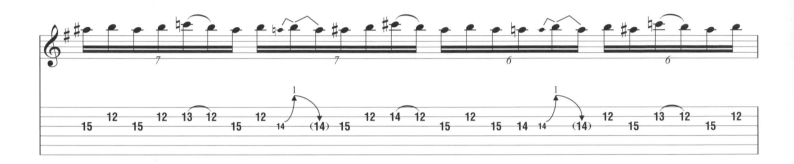

Fmaj7#11

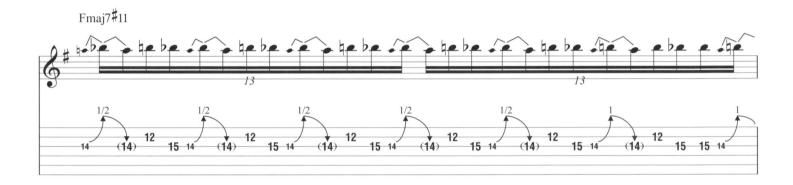

Em(add9)

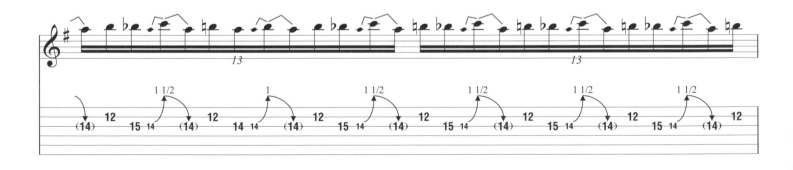

G

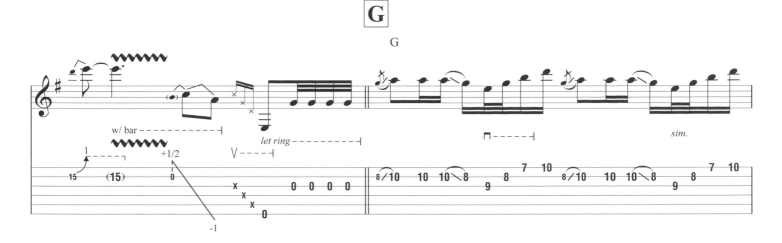

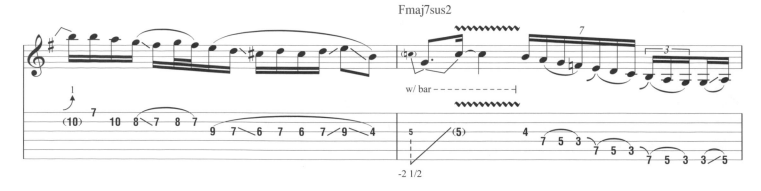

Fmaj7sus2

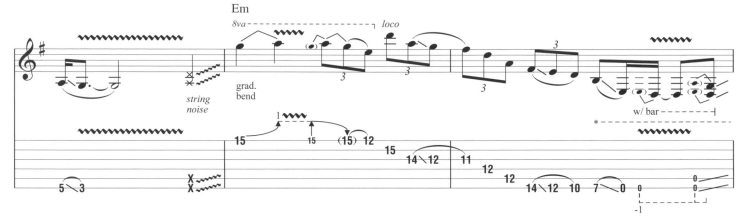

Em

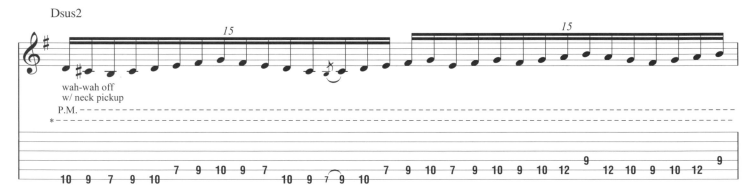

Dsus2

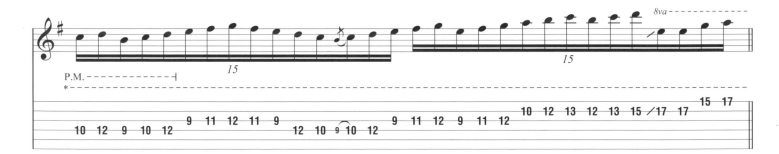

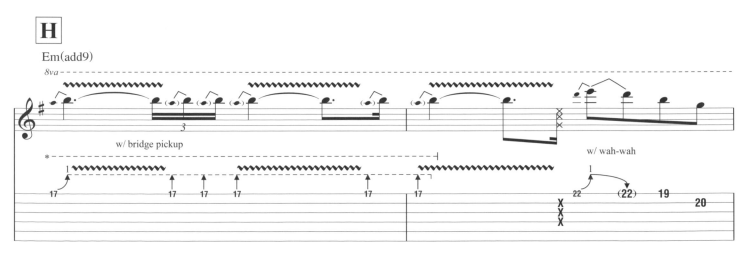

H

Em(add9)

I

Em(add9)

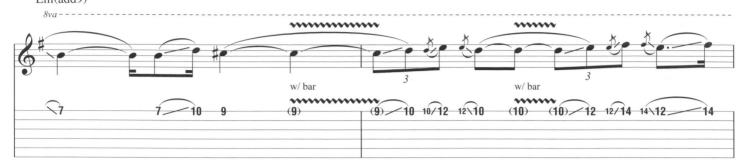

Free time

N.C.(Em)

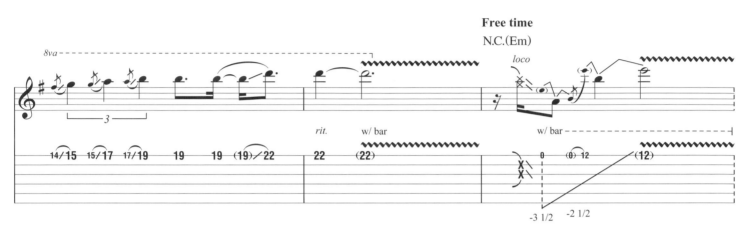

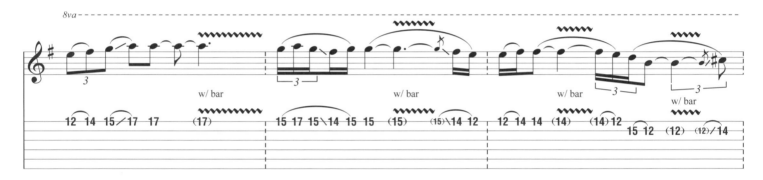

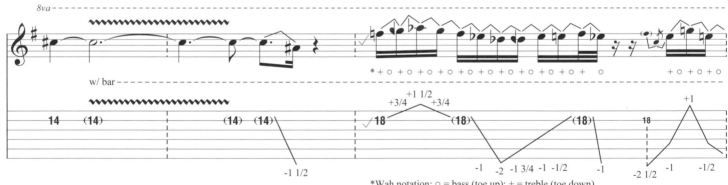

*Wah notation: ○ = bass (toe up); + = treble (toe down)

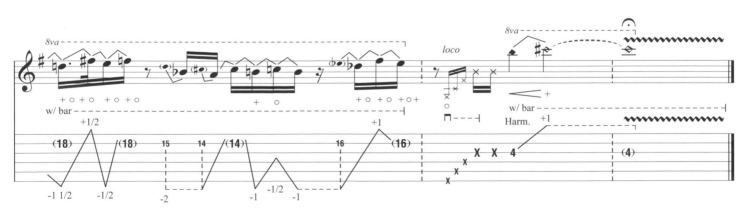

I Would Love To

By Steve Vai

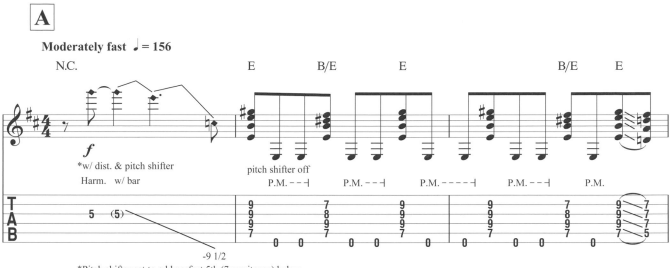

*Pitch shifter set to add perfect 5th (7 semitones) below.

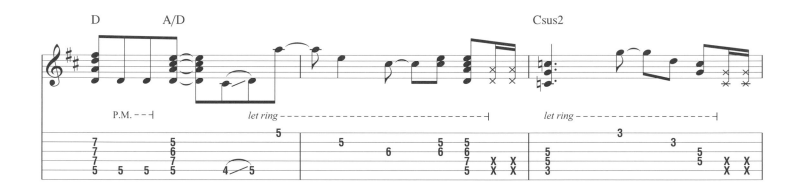

**Thumb on 6th string.

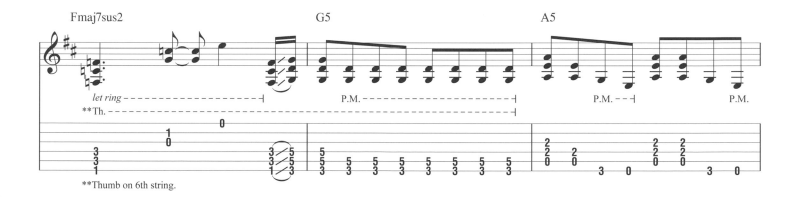

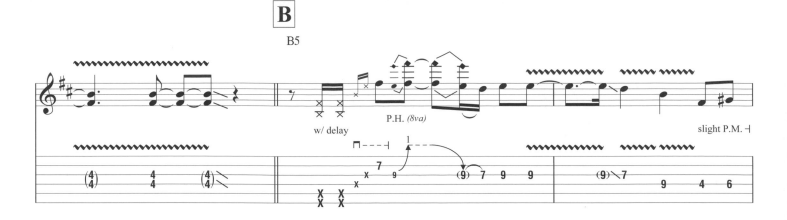

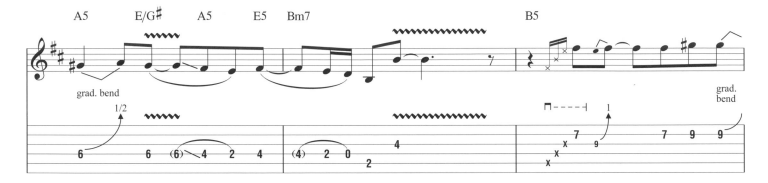

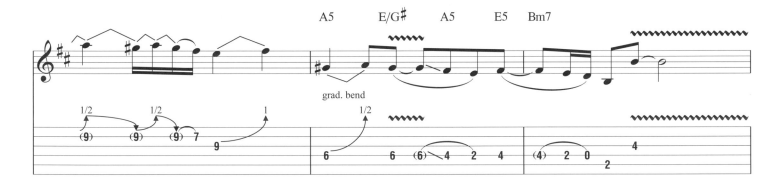

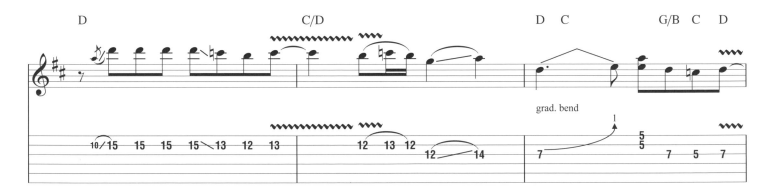

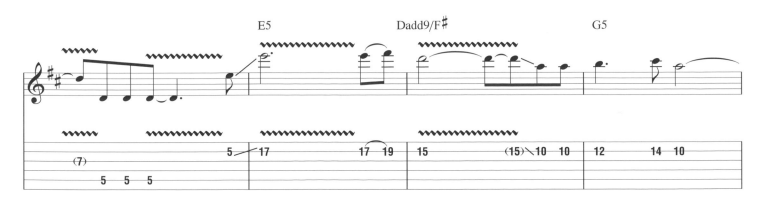

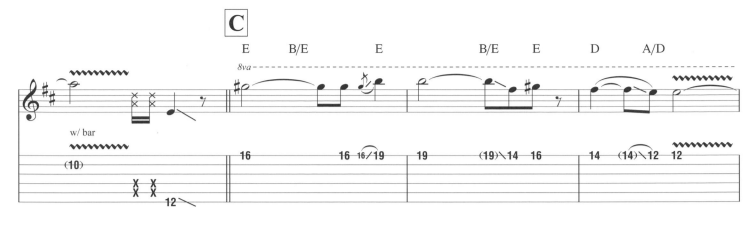

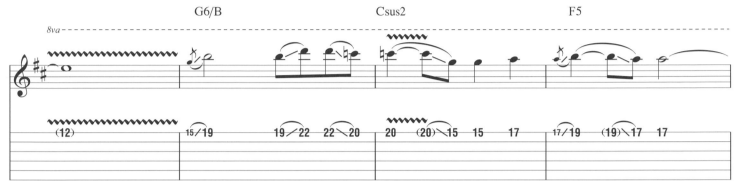

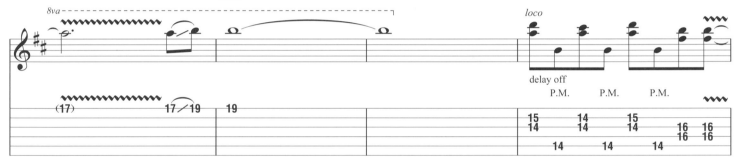

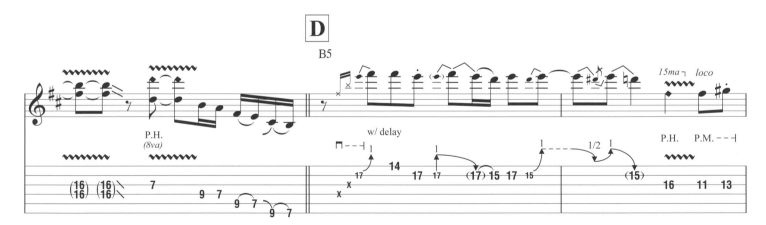

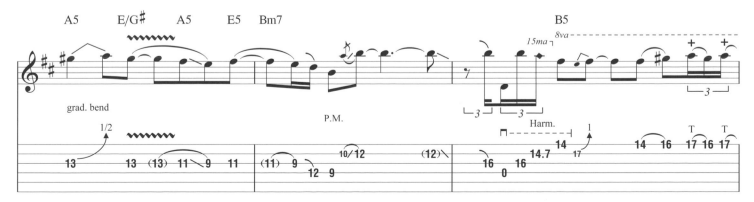

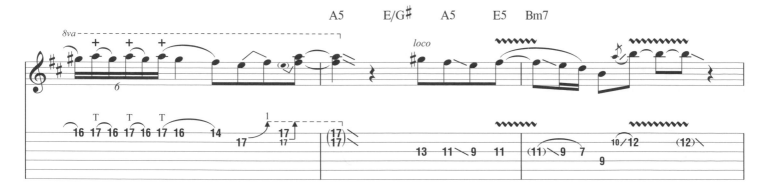

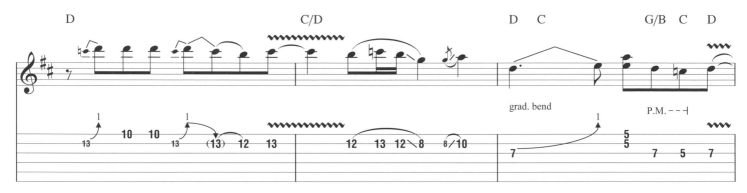

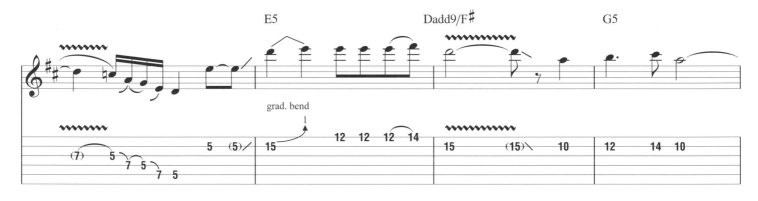

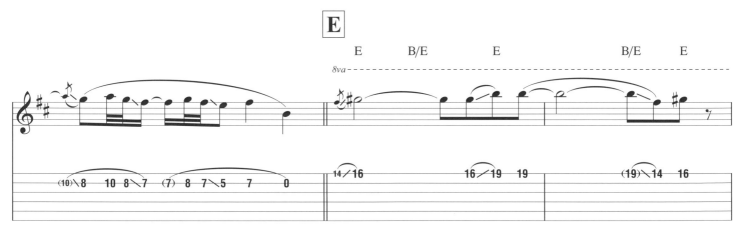

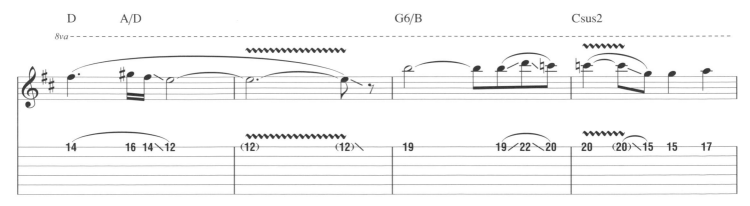

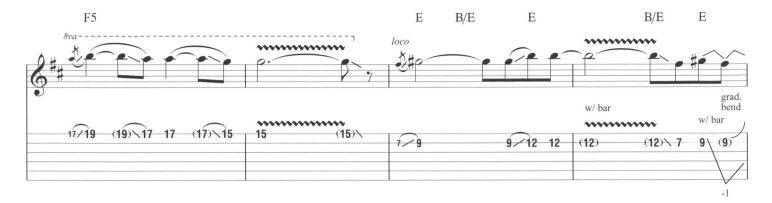

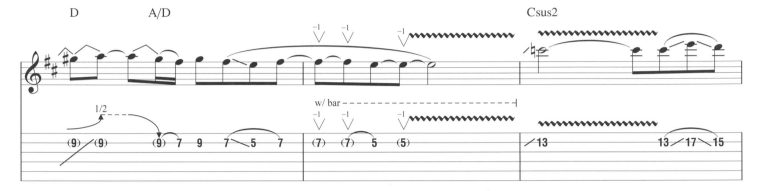

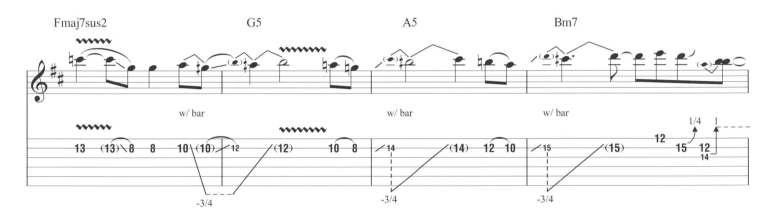

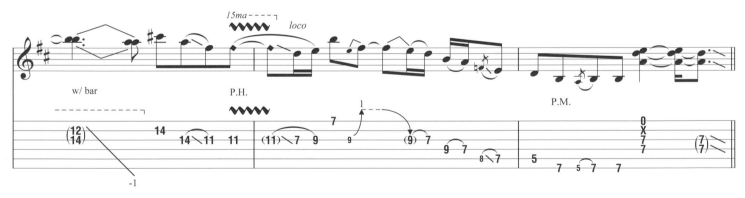

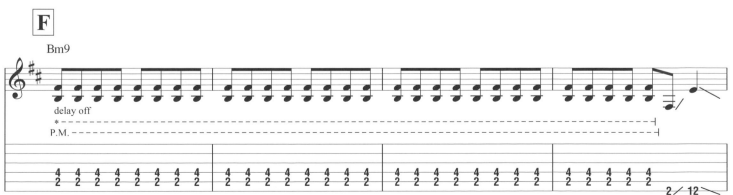

*Played 1 octave lower on 7-string gtr. on original recording.

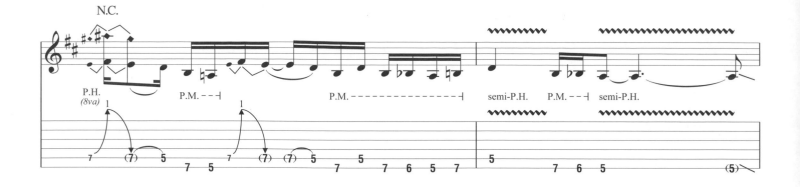

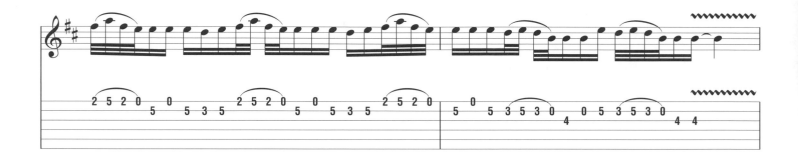

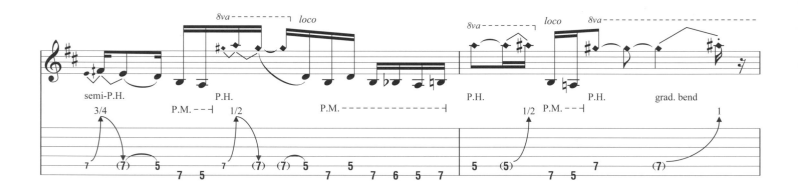

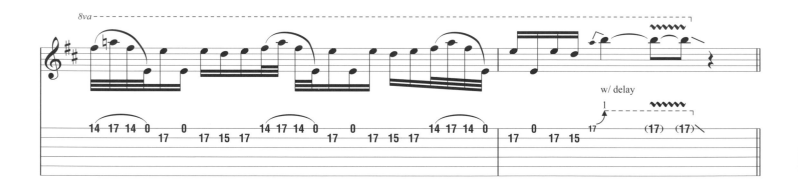

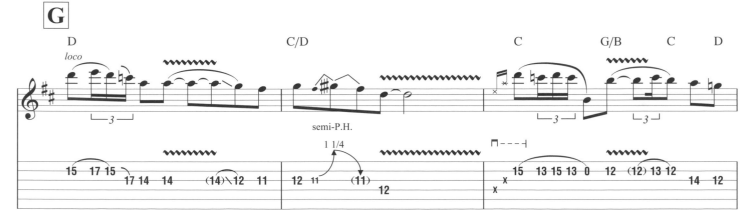

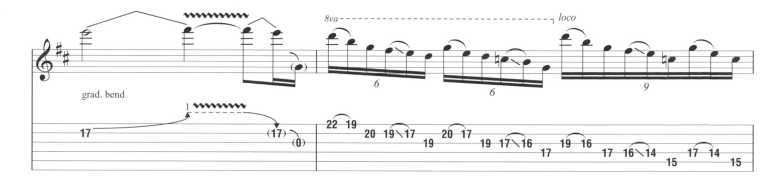

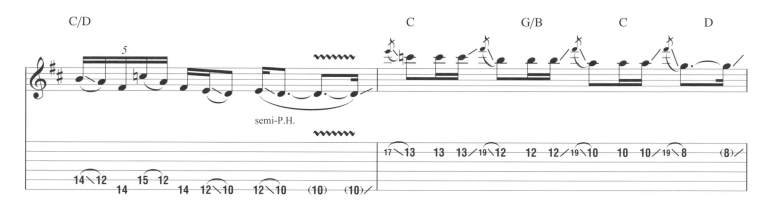

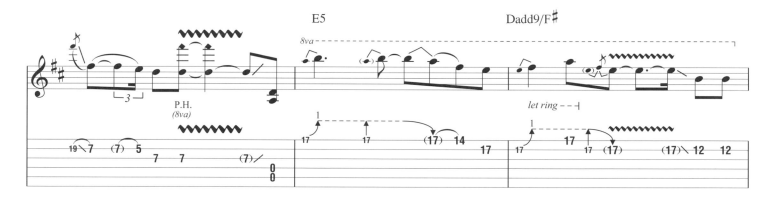

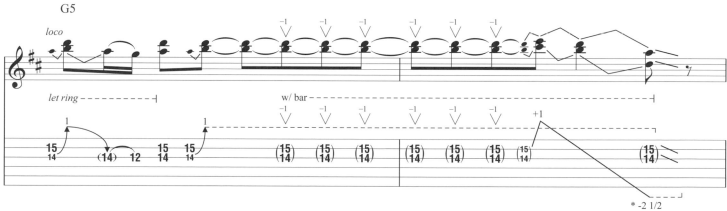

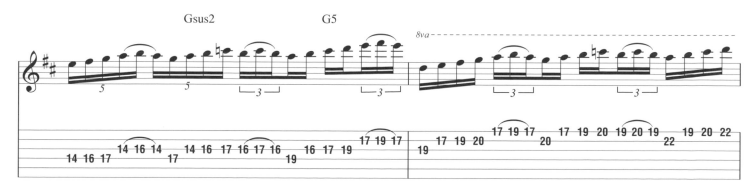

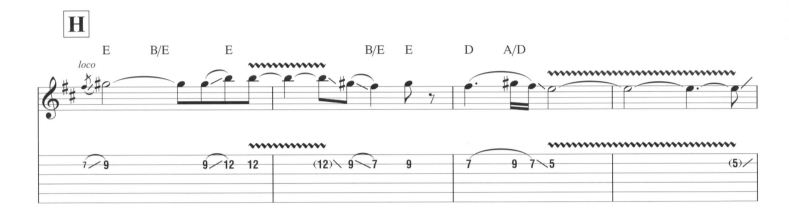

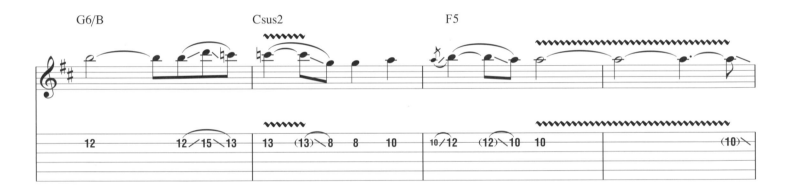

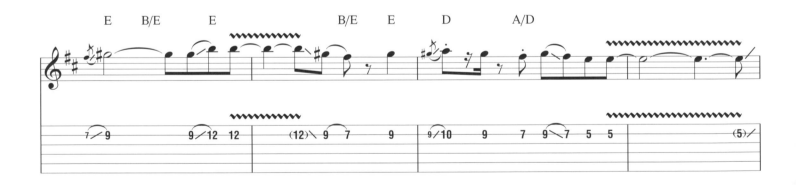

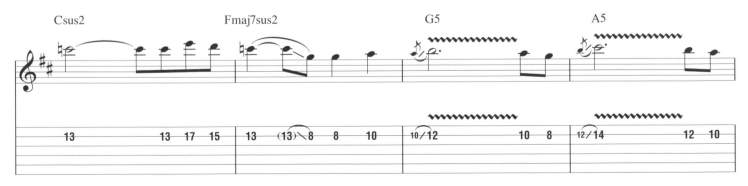

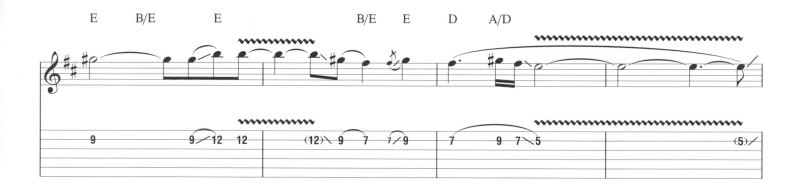

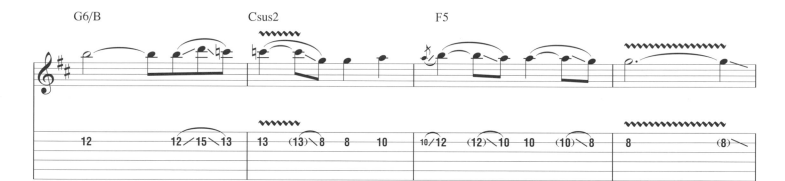

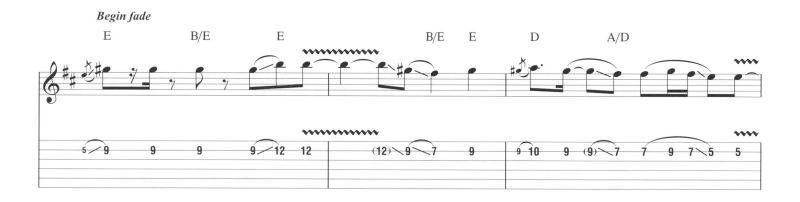

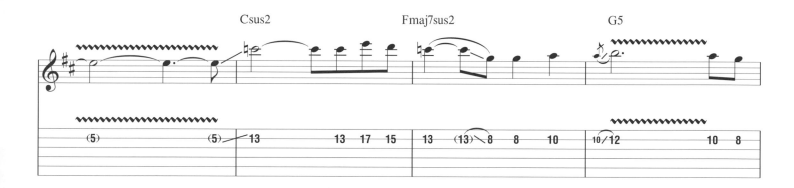

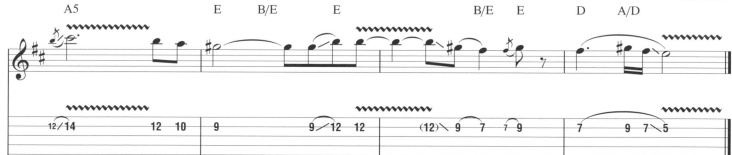

Tender Surrender

By Steve Vai

A

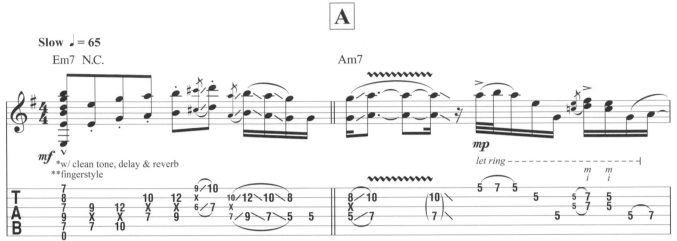

*Amp channel set for moderate dist. at full volume. Begin w/ vol. knob rolled back, pickup selector in middle + neck (coil-split) position.
Stereo delay set for 16th-note & 8th-note regeneration.
**Downstroke w/ thumb throughout when multiple notes are struck together, except where indicated.

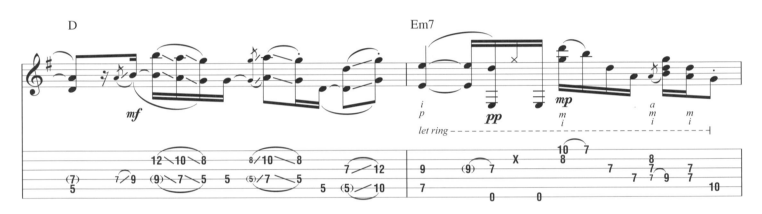

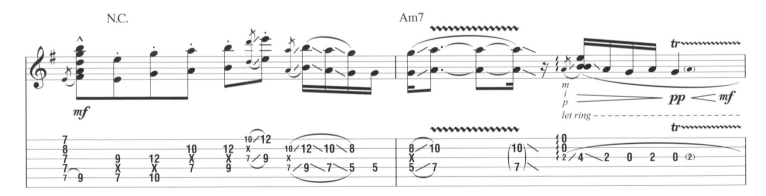

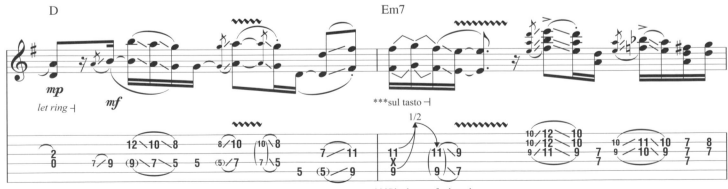

***Pluck over fretboard.

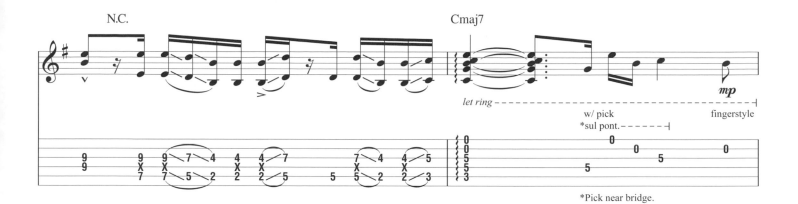

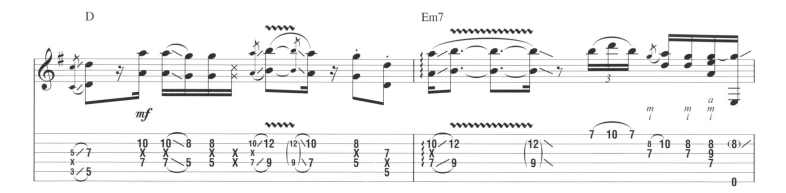

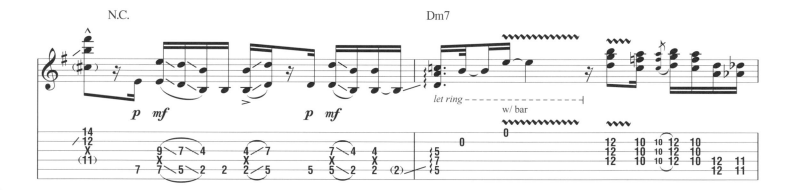

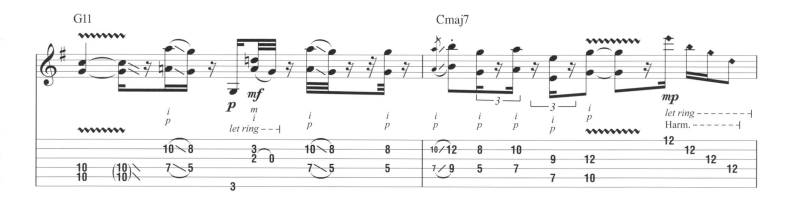

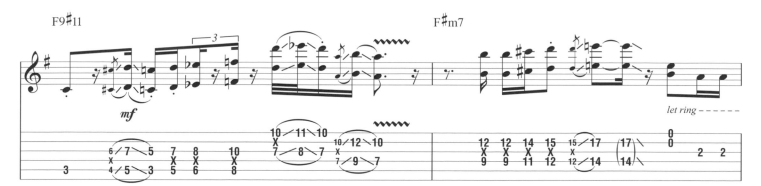

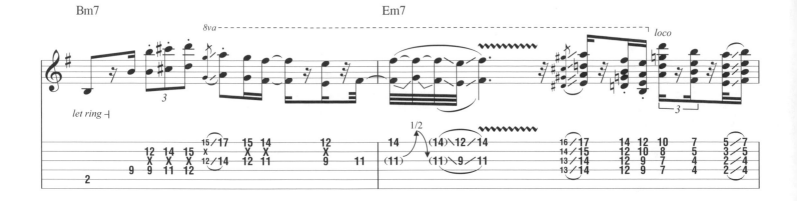

B

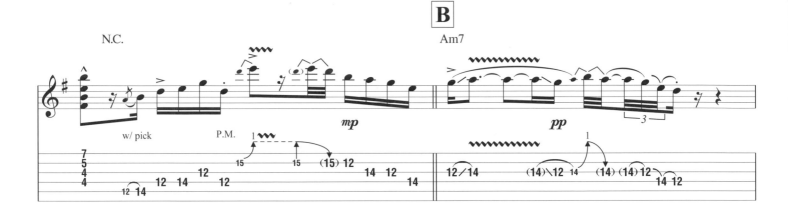

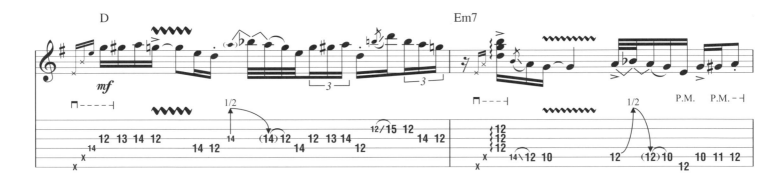

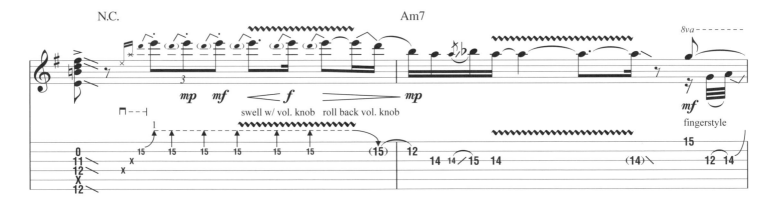

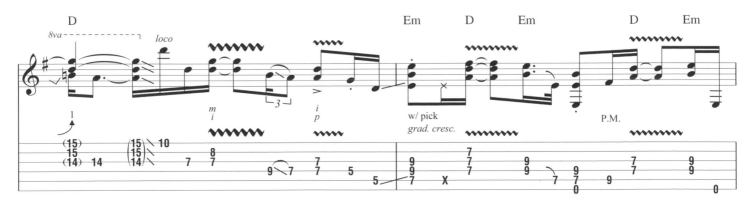

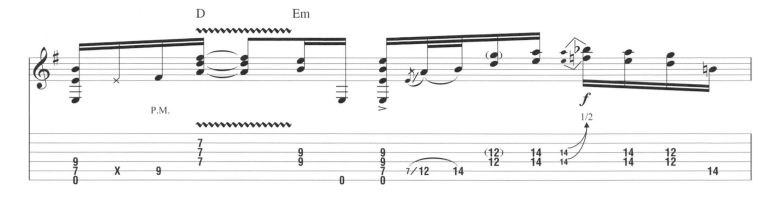

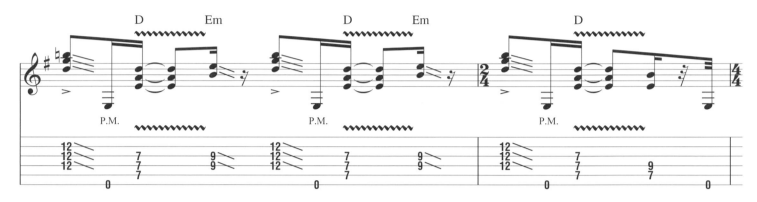

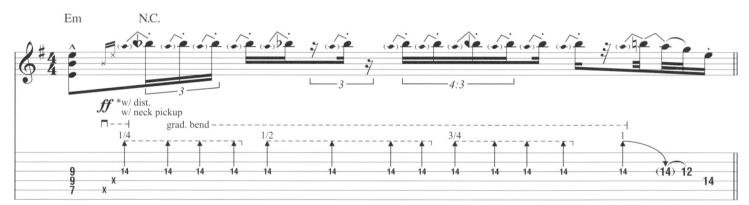

*Set vol. knob to 10, switch to higher gain channel.

C

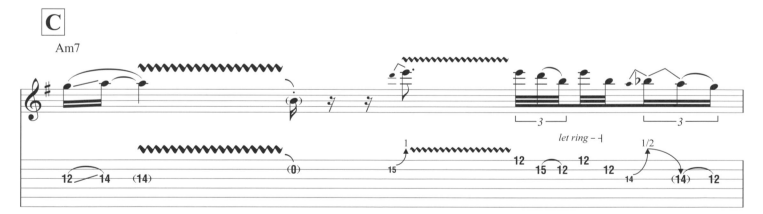

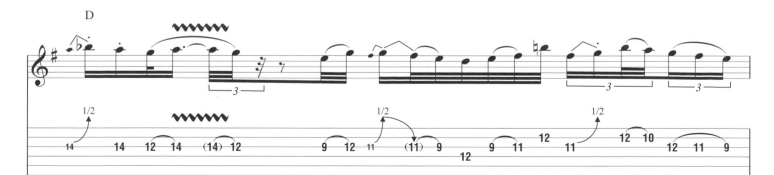

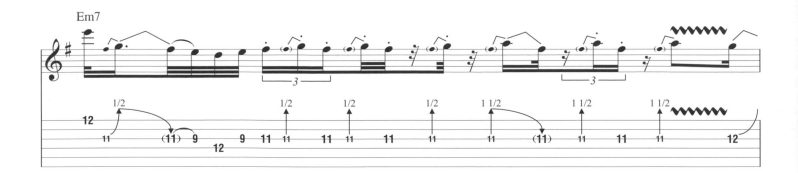

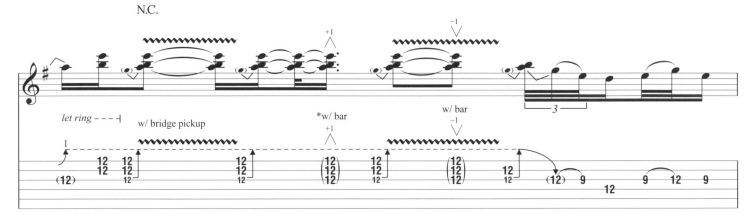

*Bar pointed toward lower strap button.

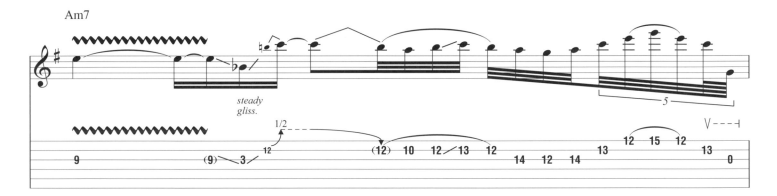

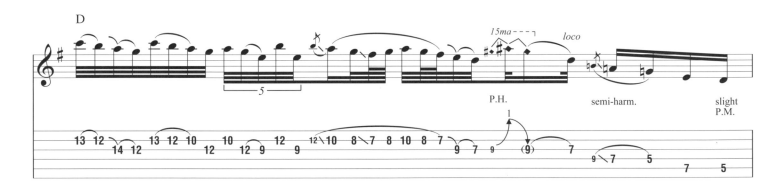

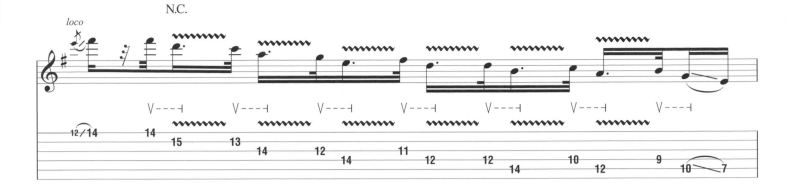

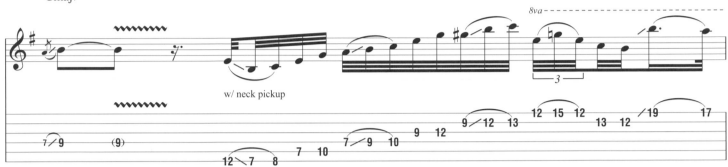

w/ neck pickup

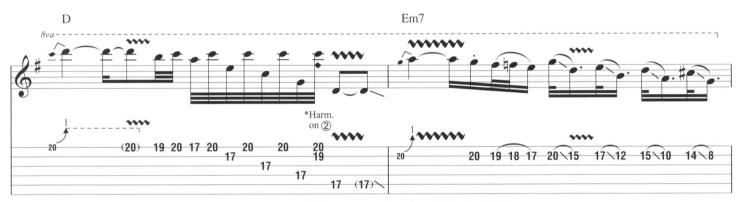

*Harm.
on ②

*4th finger touches 2nd string while fretting 1st string.

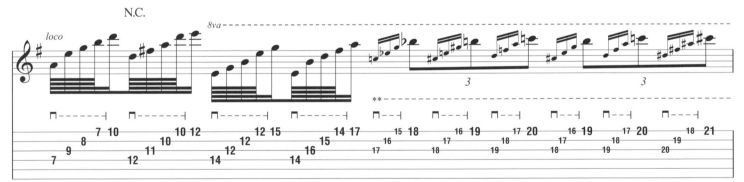

**Grace notes played ahead of beat.

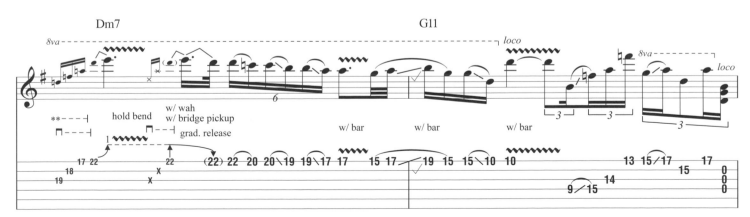

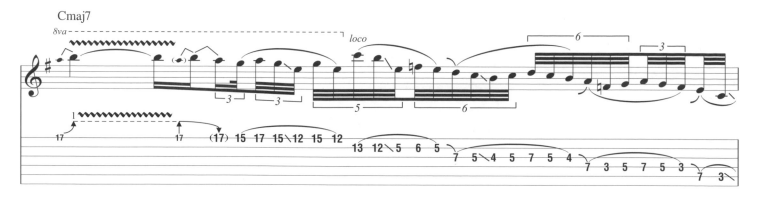

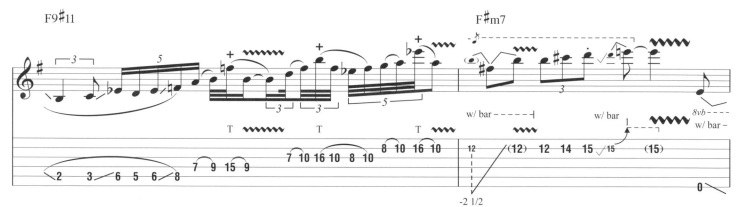

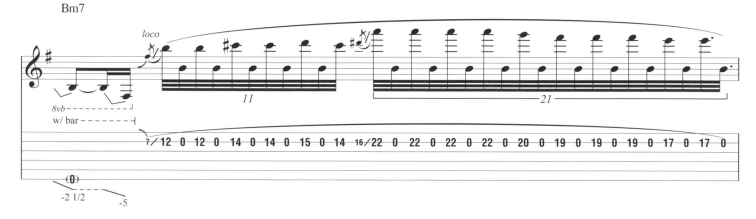

*Fret w/ R.H. middle finger.

**Bar pointed toward lower strap button.

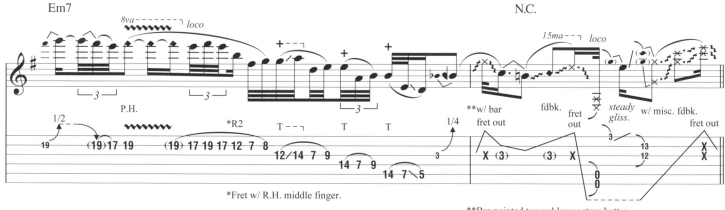

D

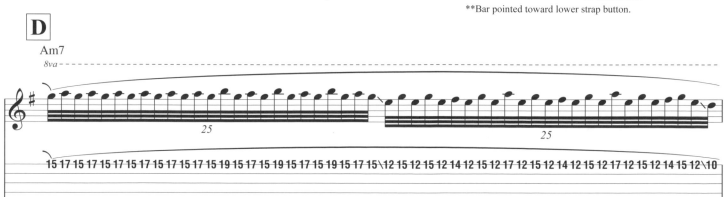

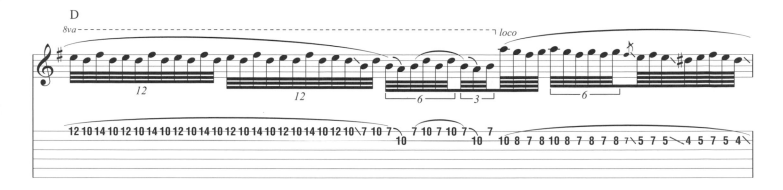

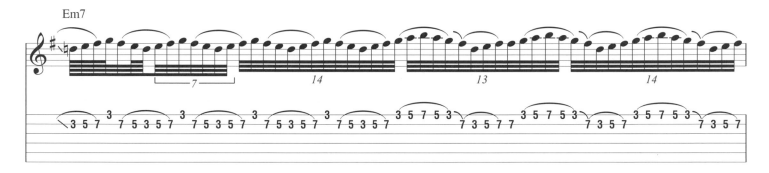

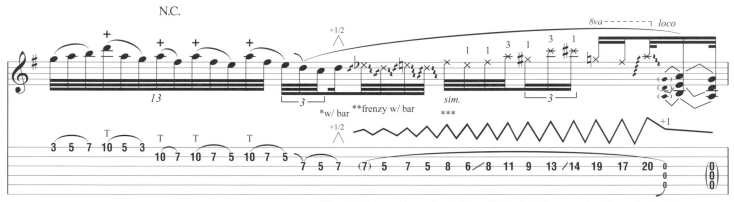

*Bar pointed toward lower strap button.   ***Begin sliding up neck while continuing to hammer on
**Shake bar w/ gradually increasing width.   and pull off w/ 3rd finger. Tab numbers indicate
fretted note at top of each vibrato cycle.

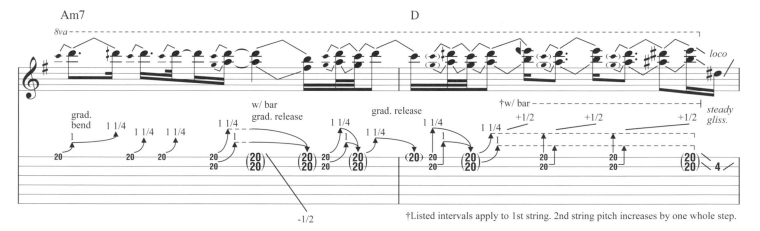

†Listed intervals apply to 1st string. 2nd string pitch increases by one whole step.

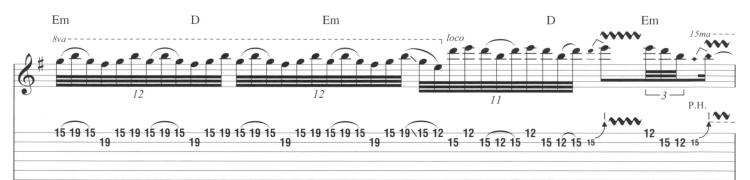

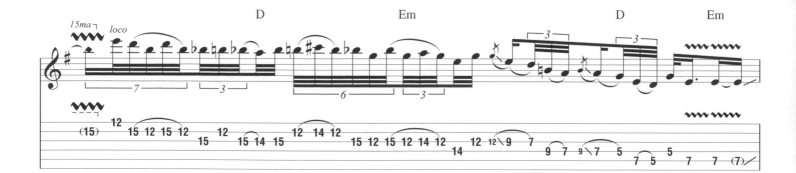

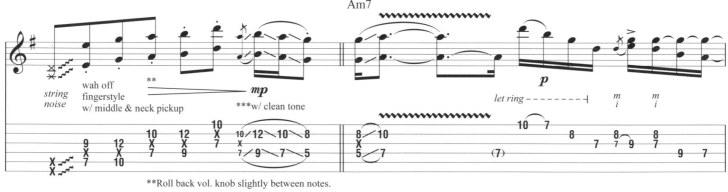

*Fretted gliss. w/ pick on 6th string.

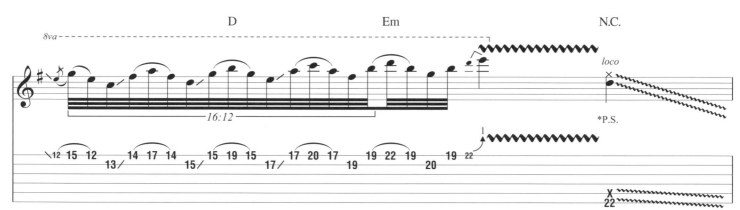

**Roll back vol. knob slightly between notes.
***As before

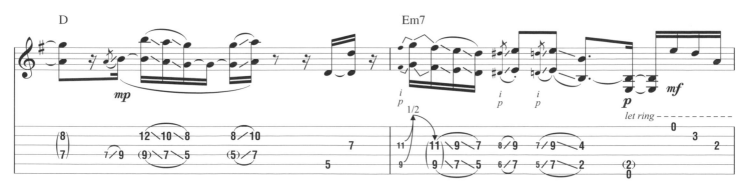

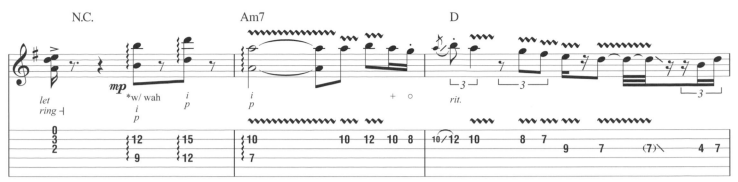

*Next 7 measures: rock wah forward & back with each note, except where indicated.
Wah notation: ○ = bass (toe up); + = treble (toe down)

Free time, Slow

N.C.

Faster

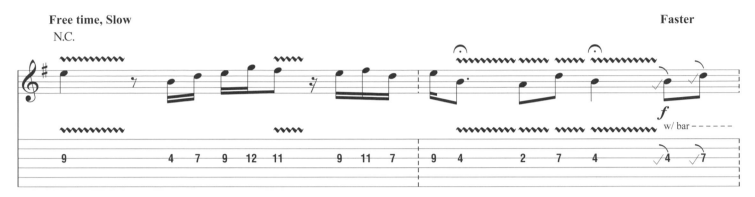

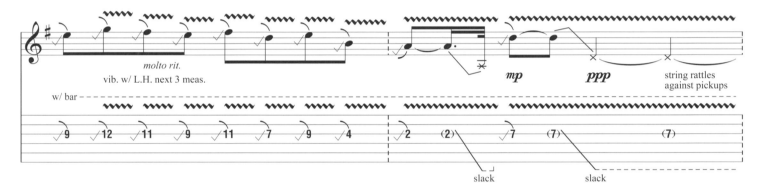

Faster

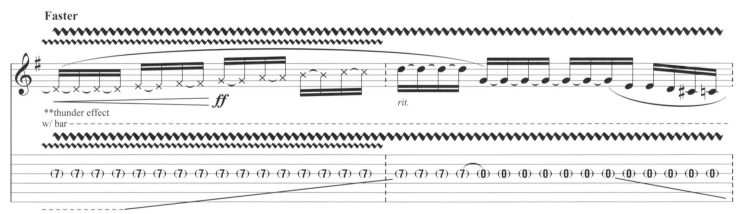

**Shake bar in rhythm shown, increasing width until reaching "0" pitch at top, then gradually diving. Allow 4th-6th strings to hit pickups and ring, next 2 meas.

Em11

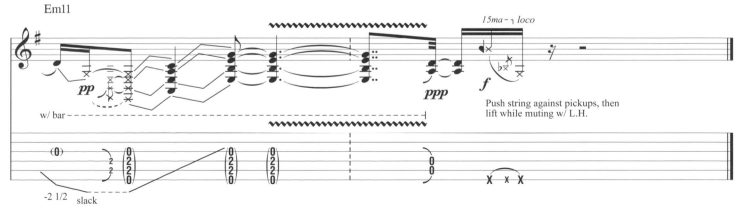

Touching Tongues

By Steve Vai

*Note played one octave lower on 7-string gtr. on original recording.

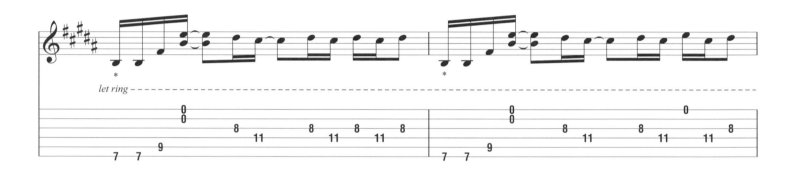

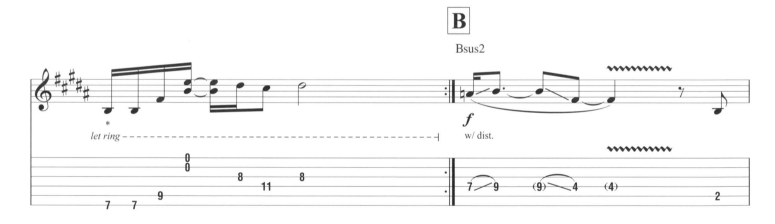

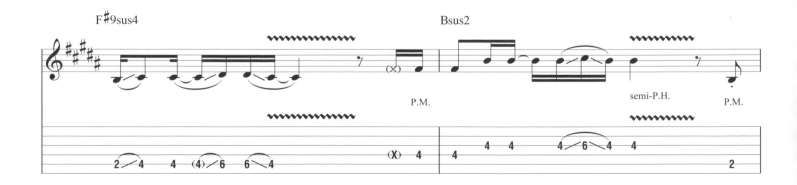

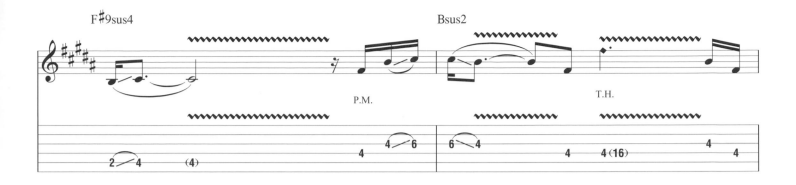

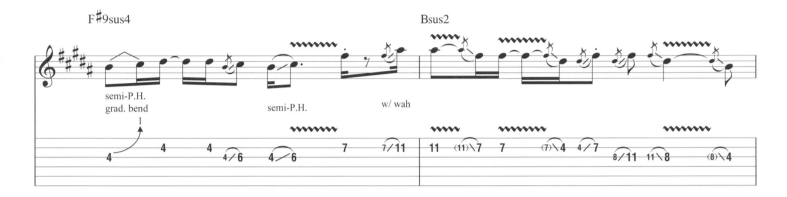

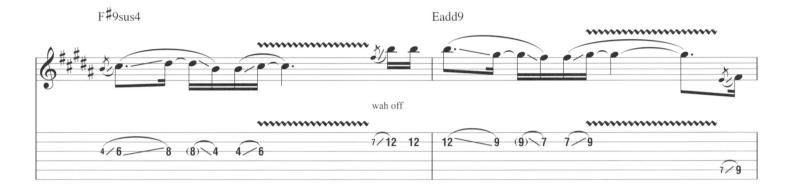

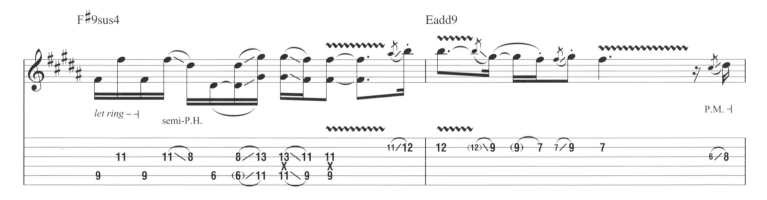

C

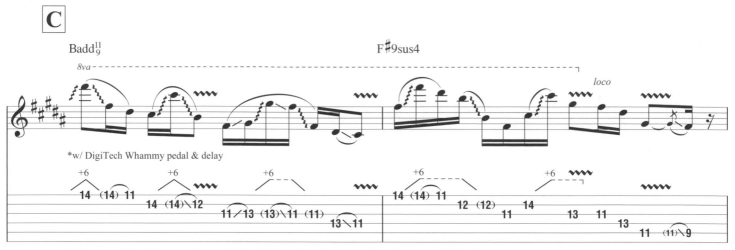

*Whammy pedal set for one octave up. Delay set for quarter-note regeneration w/ one repeat, 50% mix.

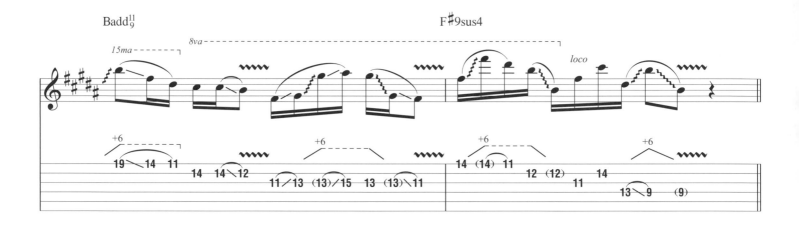

D

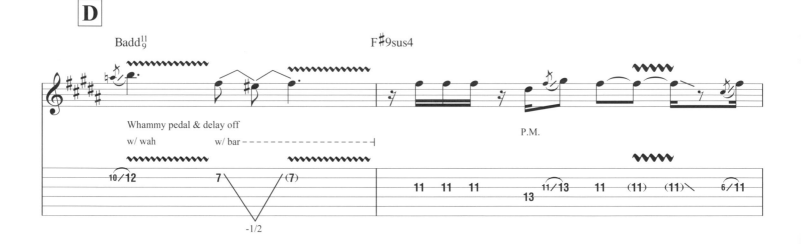

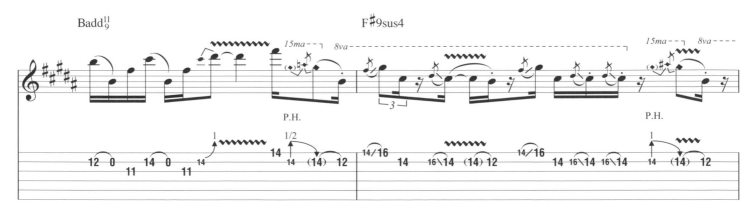

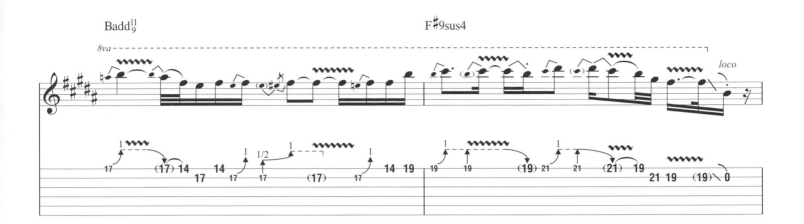

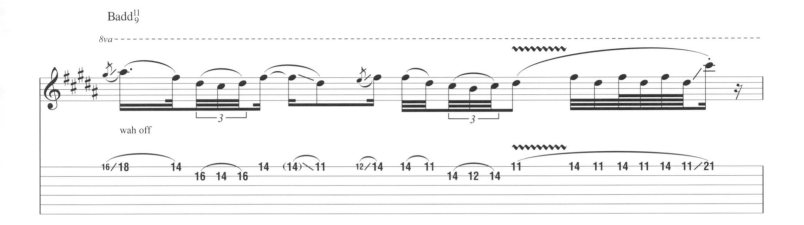

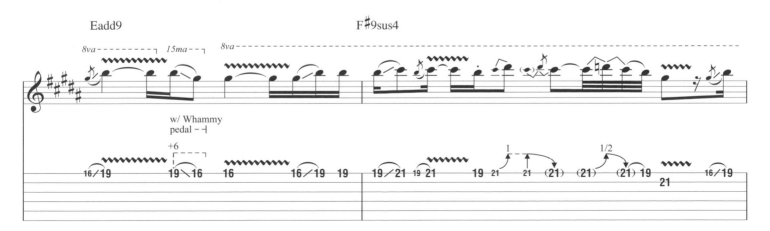

E

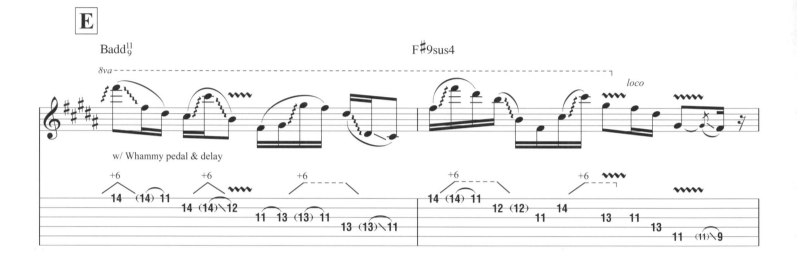

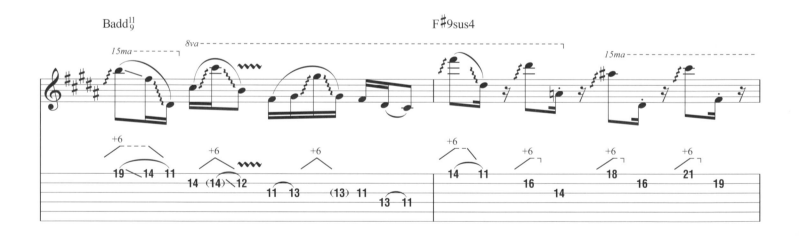

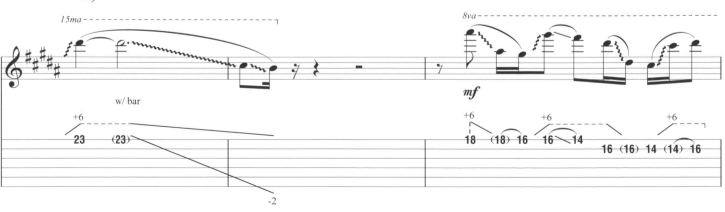

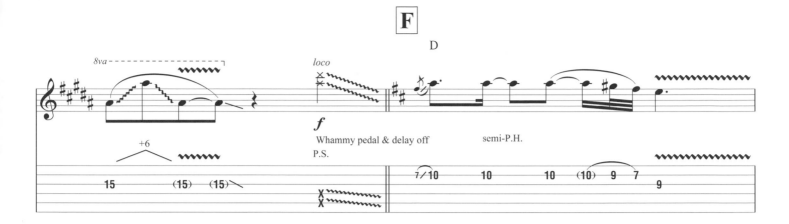

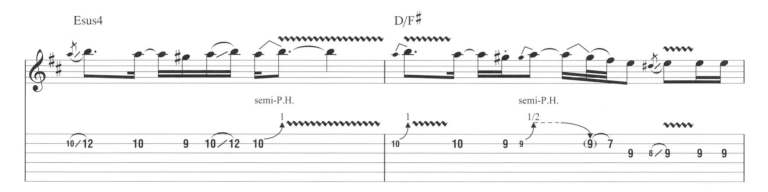

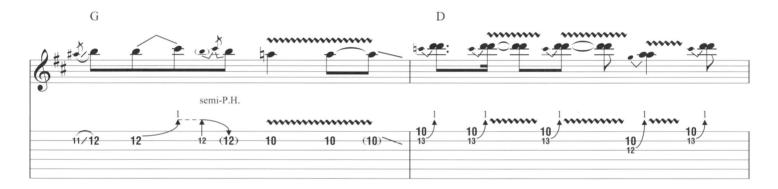

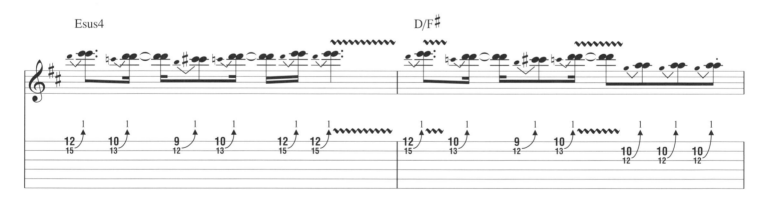

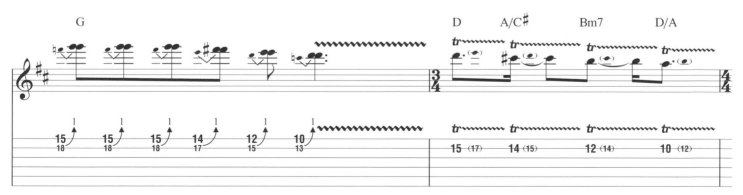

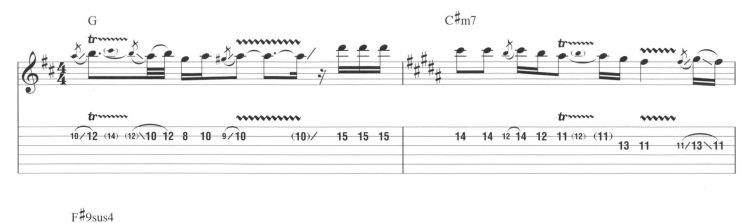

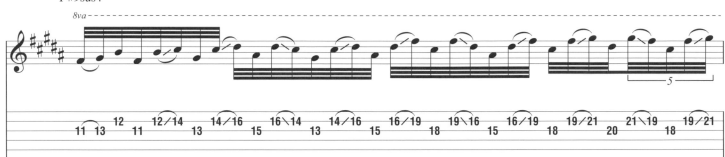

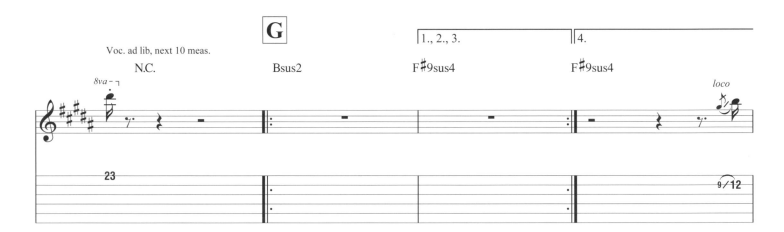

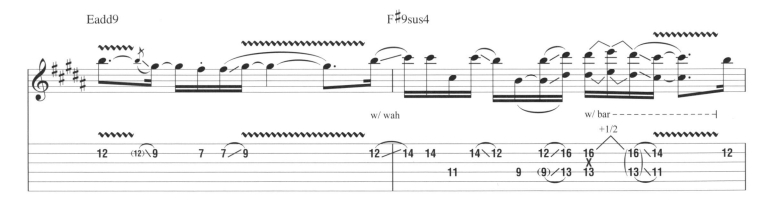

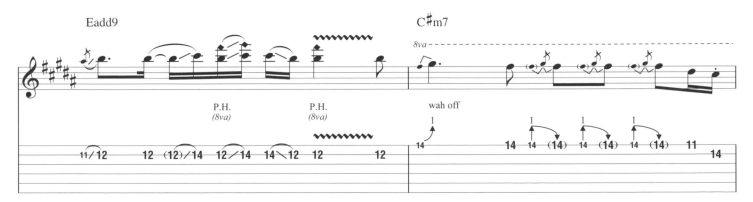

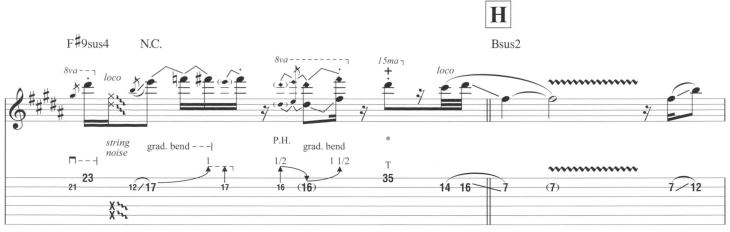

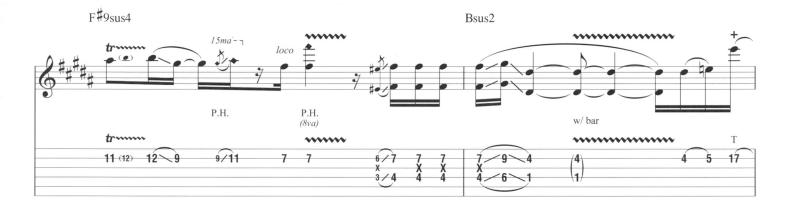

*Press string against middle pickup.

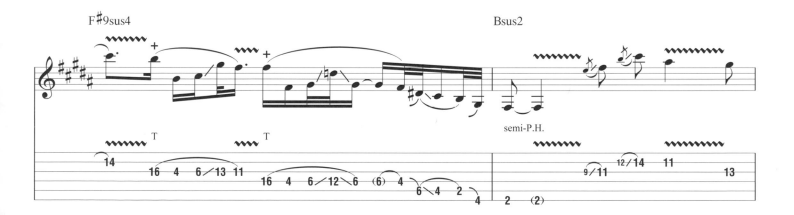

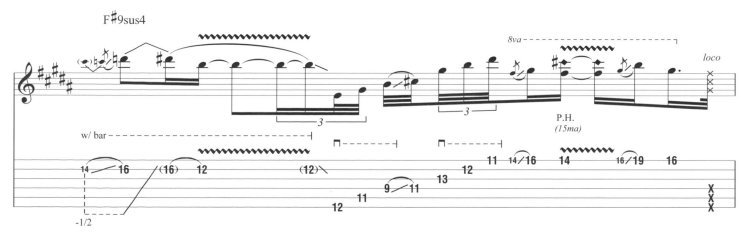

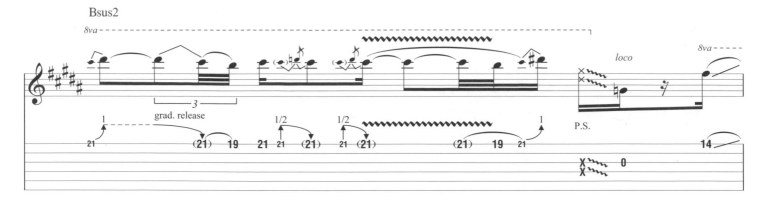

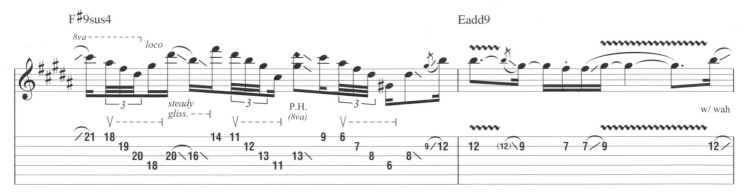

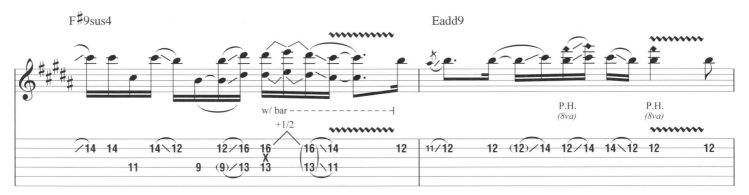

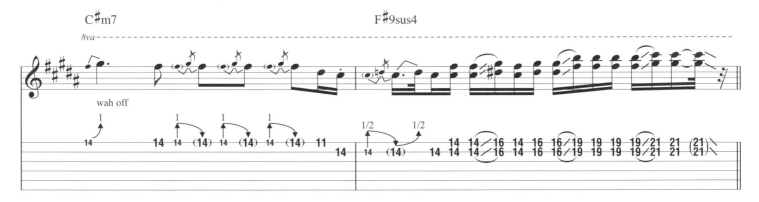

I

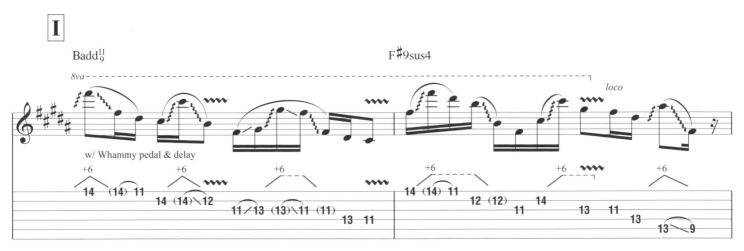

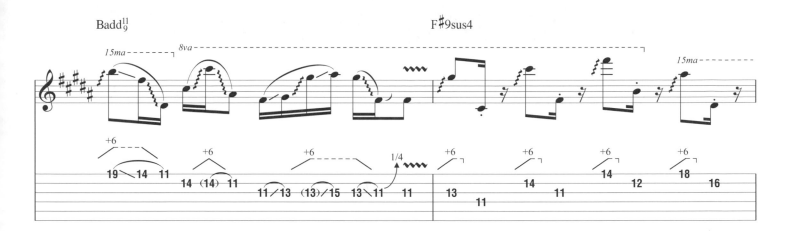

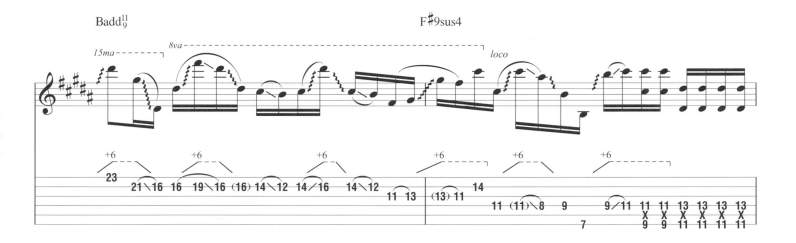

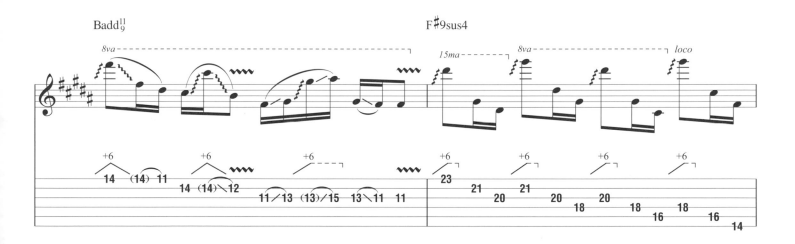

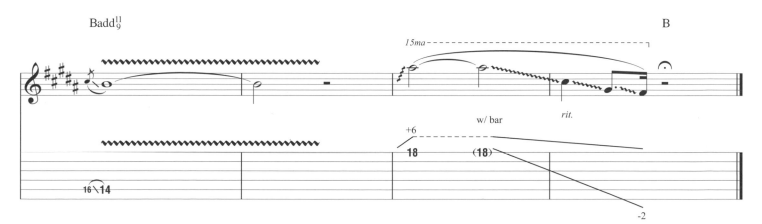

Sunshine Electric Raindrops

By Steve Vai

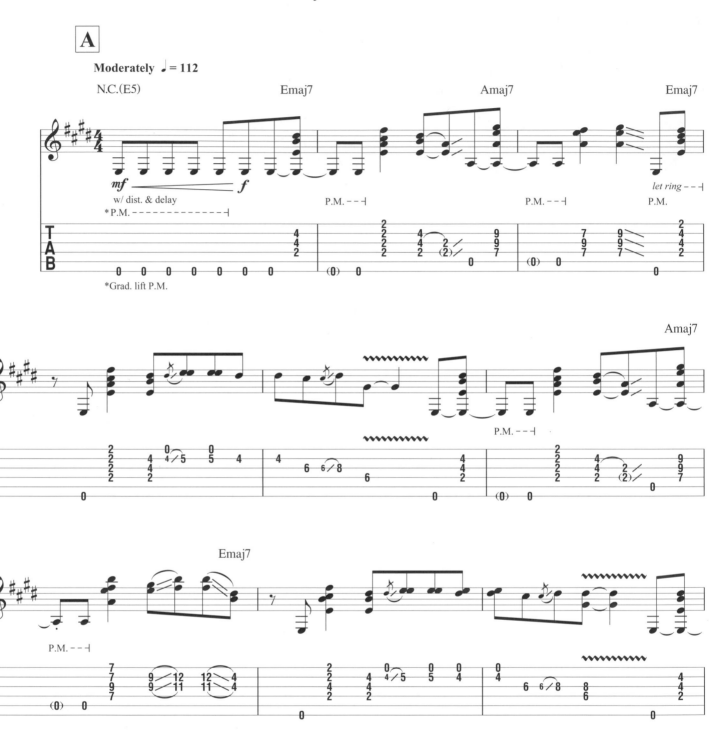

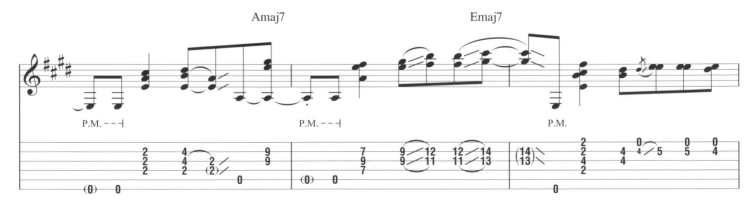

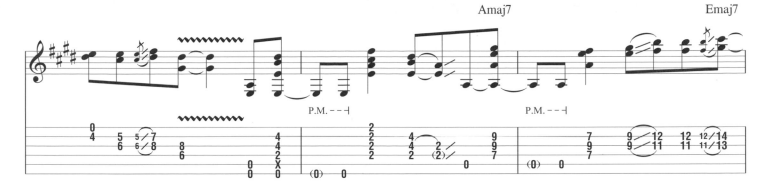

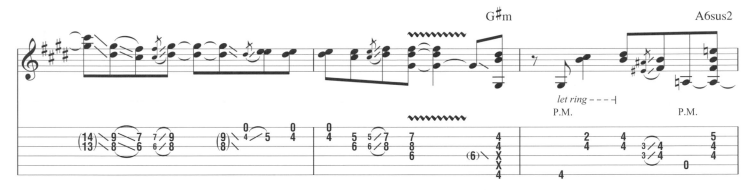

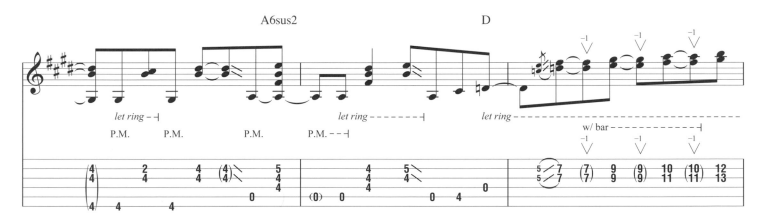

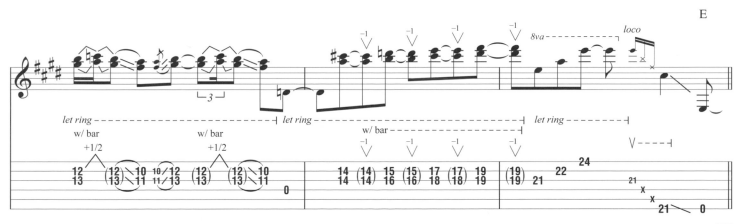

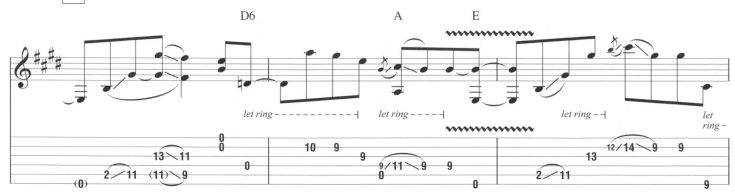

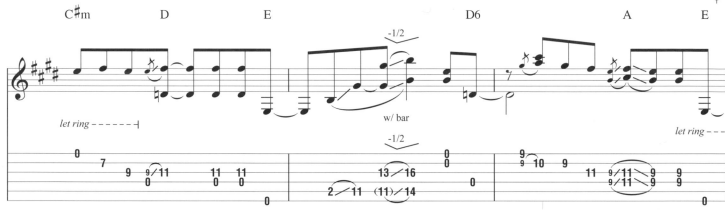

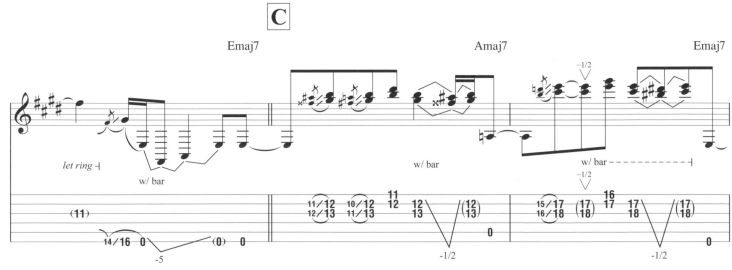

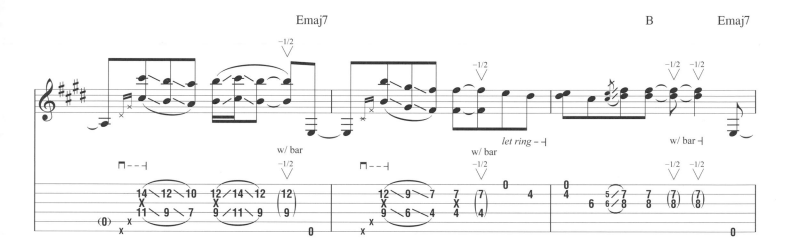

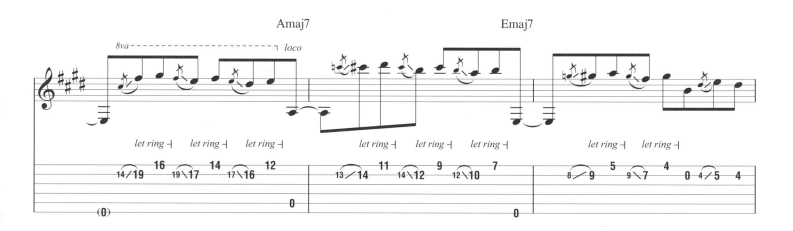

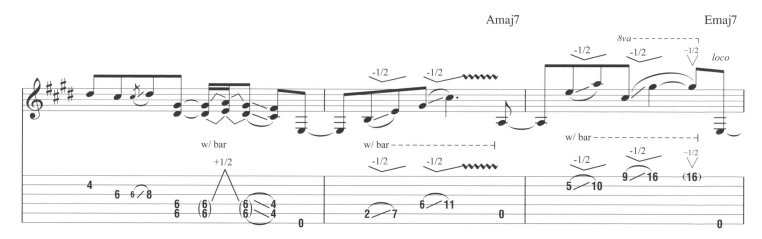

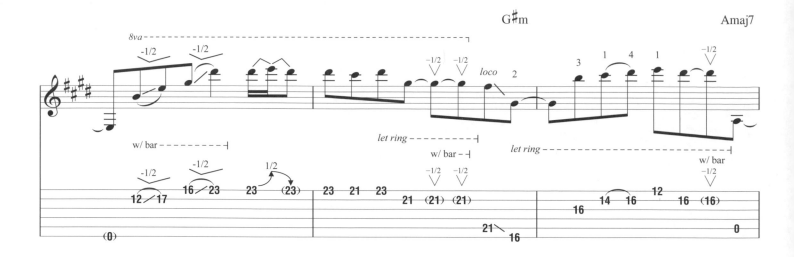

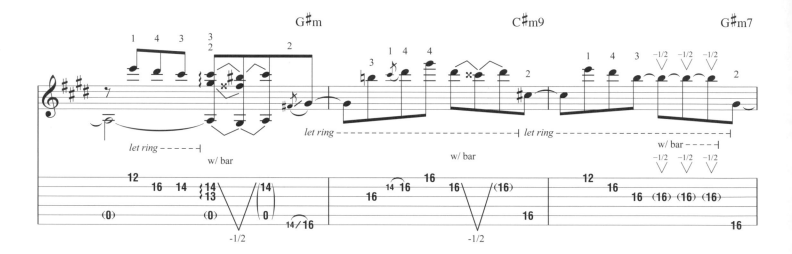

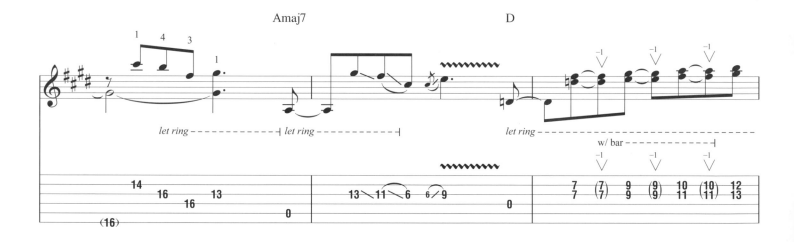

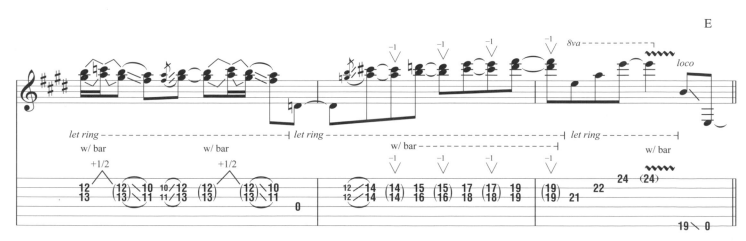

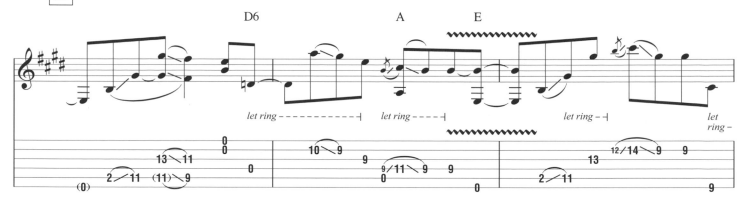

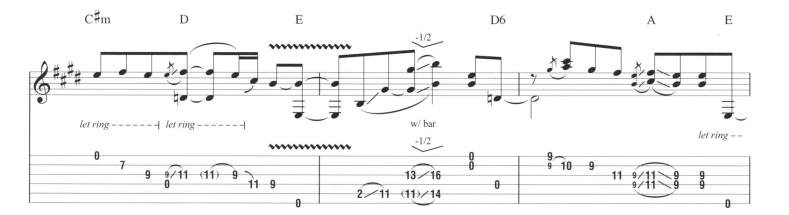

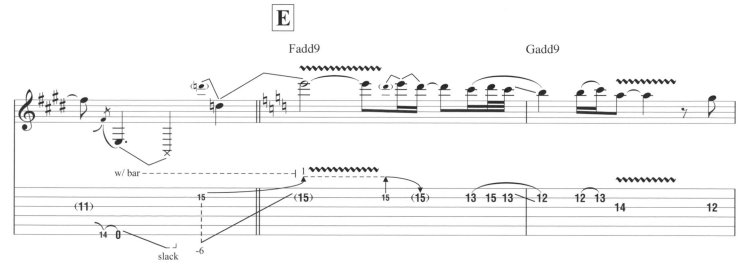

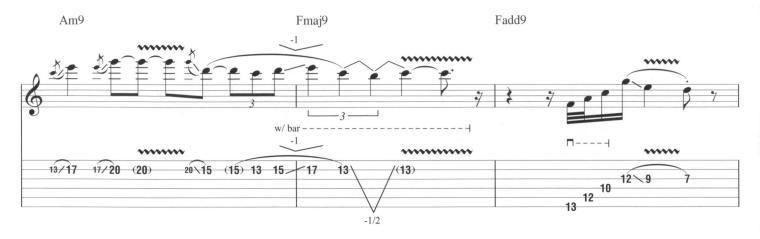

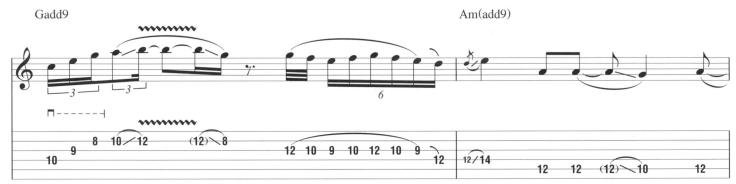

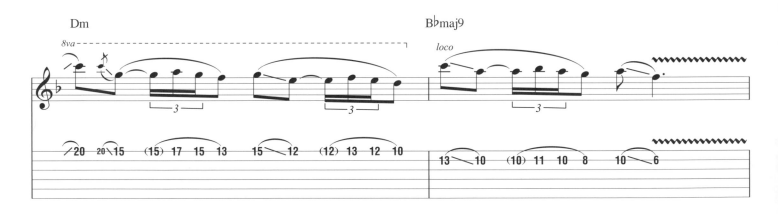

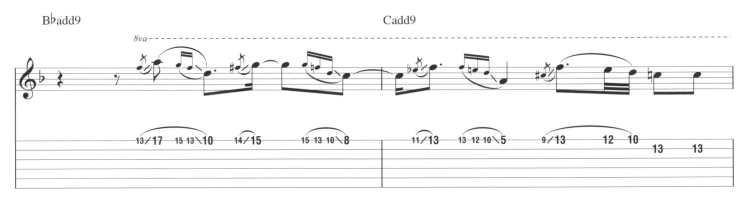

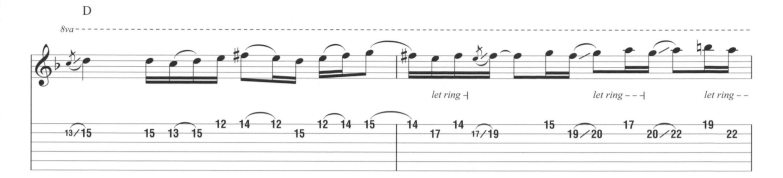

D.S. al Coda

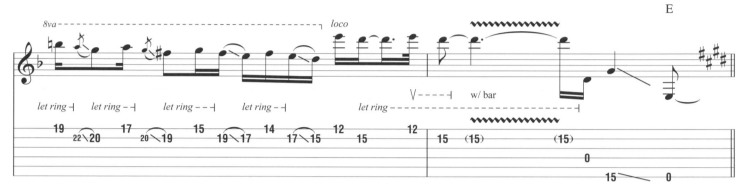

Coda

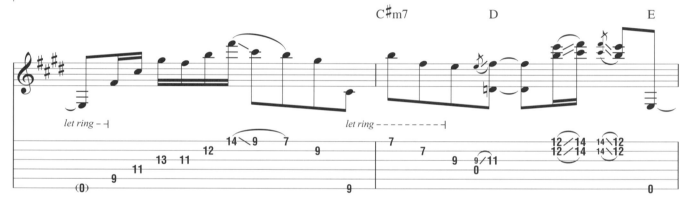

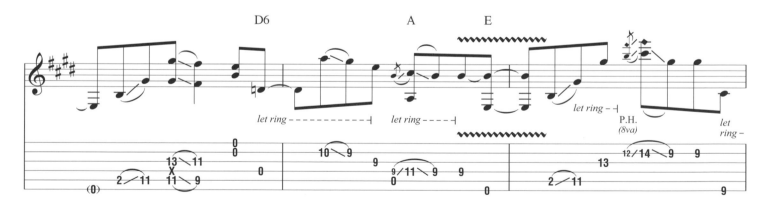

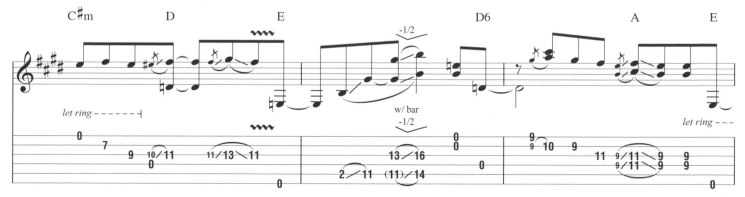

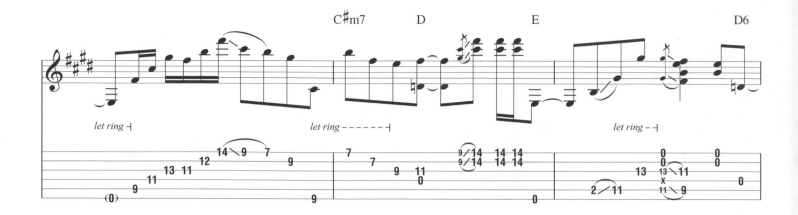

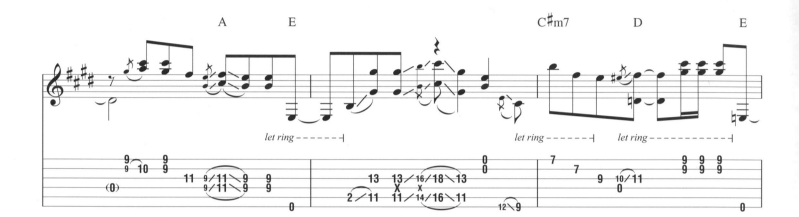

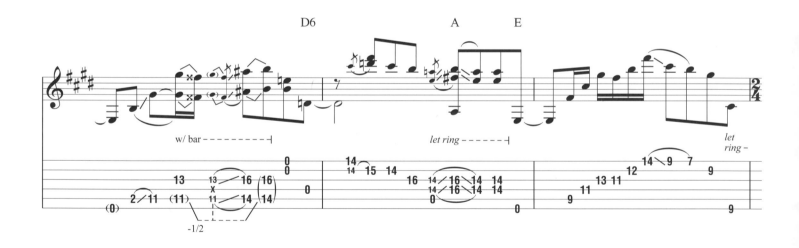

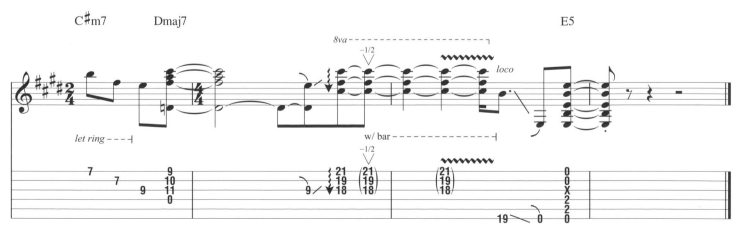

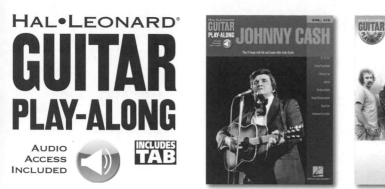

Hal•Leonard® GUITAR PLAY-ALONG

AUDIO ACCESS INCLUDED

INCLUDES TAB

This series will help you play your favorite songs quickly and easily. Just follow the tab and listen to the CD or online audio to hear how the guitar should sound, and then play along using the separate backing tracks. Playback tools are provided for slowing down the tempo without changing pitch and looping challenging parts. The melody and lyrics are included in the book so that you can sing or simply follow along.

89. REGGAE
00700468 .... $15.99

90. CLASSICAL POP
00700469 .... $14.99

91. BLUES INSTRUMENTALS
00700505 .... $17.99

92. EARLY ROCK INSTRUMENTALS
00700506 .... $15.99

93. ROCK INSTRUMENTALS
00700507 .... $16.99

94. SLOW BLUES
00700508 .... $16.99

95. BLUES CLASSICS
00700509 .... $15.99

96. BEST COUNTRY HITS
00211615 .... $16.99

97. CHRISTMAS CLASSICS
00236542 .... $14.99

98. ROCK BAND
00700704 .... $14.95

99. ZZ TOP
00700762 .... $16.99

100. B.B. KING
00700466 .... $16.99

101. SONGS FOR BEGINNERS
00701917 .... $14.99

102. CLASSIC PUNK
00700769 .... $14.99

103. SWITCHFOOT
00700773 .... $16.99

104. DUANE ALLMAN
00700846 .... $16.99

105. LATIN
00700939 .... $16.99

106. WEEZER
00700958 .... $14.99

107. CREAM
00701069 .... $16.99

108. THE WHO
00701053 .... $16.99

109. STEVE MILLER
00701054 .... $17.99

110. SLIDE GUITAR HITS
00701055 .... $16.99

111. JOHN MELLENCAMP
00701056 .... $14.99

112. QUEEN
00701052 .... $16.99

113. JIM CROCE
00701058 .... $17.99

114. BON JOVI
00701060 .... $16.99

115. JOHNNY CASH
00701070 .... $16.99

116. THE VENTURES
00701124 .... $16.99

117. BRAD PAISLEY
00701224 .... $16.99

118. ERIC JOHNSON
00701353 .... $16.99

119. AC/DC CLASSICS
00701356 .... $17.99

120. PROGRESSIVE ROCK
00701457 .... $14.99

121. U2
00701508 .... $16.99

122. CROSBY, STILLS & NASH
00701610 .... $16.99

123. LENNON & MCCARTNEY ACOUSTIC
00701614 .... $16.99

125. JEFF BECK
00701687 .... $16.99

126. BOB MARLEY
00701701 .... $16.99

127. 1970S ROCK
00701739 .... $16.99

128. 1960S ROCK
00701740 .... $14.99

129. MEGADETH
00701741 .... $16.99

130. IRON MAIDEN
00701742 .... $17.99

131. 1990S ROCK
00701743 .... $14.99

132. COUNTRY ROCK
00701757 .... $15.99

133. TAYLOR SWIFT
00701894 .... $16.99

134. AVENGED SEVENFOLD
00701906 .... $16.99

135. MINOR BLUES
00151350 .... $17.99

136. GUITAR THEMES
00701922 .... $14.99

137. IRISH TUNES
00701966 .... $15.99

138. BLUEGRASS CLASSICS
00701967 .... $16.99

139. GARY MOORE
00702370 .... $16.99

140. MORE STEVIE RAY VAUGHAN
00702396 .... $17.99

141. ACOUSTIC HITS
00702401 .... $16.99

142. GEORGE HARRISON
00237697 .... $17.99

143. SLASH
00702425 .... $19.99

144. DJANGO REINHARDT
00702531 .... $16.99

145. DEF LEPPARD
00702532 .... $17.99

146. ROBERT JOHNSON
00702533 .... $16.99

147. SIMON & GARFUNKEL
14041591 .... $16.99

148. BOB DYLAN
14041592 .... $16.99

149. AC/DC HITS
14041593 .... $17.99

150. ZAKK WYLDE
02501717 .... $16.99

151. J.S. BACH
02501730 .... $16.99

152. JOE BONAMASSA
02501751 .... $19.99

153. RED HOT CHILI PEPPERS
00702990 .... $19.99

155. ERIC CLAPTON – FROM THE ALBUM UNPLUGGED
00703085 .... $16.99

156. SLAYER
00703770 .... $17.99

157. FLEETWOOD MAC
00101382 .... $16.99

159. WES MONTGOMERY
00102593 .... $19.99

160. T-BONE WALKER
00102641 .... $17.99

161. THE EAGLES – ACOUSTIC
00102659 .... $17.99

162. THE EAGLES HITS
00102667 .... $17.99

163. PANTERA
00103036 .... $17.99

164. VAN HALEN 1986-1995
00110270 .... $17.99

165. GREEN DAY
00210343 .... $17.99

166. MODERN BLUES
00700764 .... $16.99

167. DREAM THEATER
00111938 .... $24.99

168. KISS
00113421 .... $16.99

169. TAYLOR SWIFT
00115982 .... $16.99

170. THREE DAYS GRACE
00117337 .... $16.99

171. JAMES BROWN
00117420 .... $16.99

173. TRANS-SIBERIAN ORCHESTRA
00119907 .... $19.99

174. SCORPIONS
00122119 .... $16.99

175. MICHAEL SCHENKER
00122127 .... $16.99

176. BLUES BREAKERS WITH JOHN MAYALL & ERIC CLAPTON
00122132 .... $19.99

177. ALBERT KING
00123271 .... $16.99

178. JASON MRAZ
00124165 .... $17.99

179. RAMONES
00127073 .... $16.99

180. BRUNO MARS
00129706 .... $16.99

181. JACK JOHNSON
00129854 .... $16.99

182. SOUNDGARDEN
00138161 .... $17.99

183. BUDDY GUY
00138240 .... $17.99

184. KENNY WAYNE SHEPHERD
00138258 .... $17.99

185. JOE SATRIANI
00139457 .... $17.99

186. GRATEFUL DEAD
00139459 .... $17.99

187. JOHN DENVER
00140839 .... $17.99

188. MÖTLEY CRUE
00141145 .... $17.99

189. JOHN MAYER
00144350 .... $17.99

190. DEEP PURPLE
00146152 .... $17.99

191. PINK FLOYD CLASSICS
00146164 .... $17.99

192. JUDAS PRIEST
00151352 .... $17.99

193. STEVE VAI
00156028 .... $19.99

195. METALLICA: 1983-1988
00234291 .... $19.99

196. METALLICA: 1991-2016
00234292 .... $19.99

For complete songlists, visit
Hal Leonard online at
www.halleonard.com

Prices, contents, and availability subject to
change without notice.

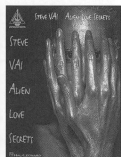

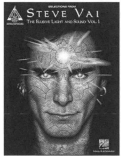

THE STORY OF LIGHT

INCLUDES TAB *The Story of Light* is the second installment in the *Real Illusions* planned trilogy, a "multi-layered melange based on the amplified mental exaggerations of a truth-seeking madman who sees the world through his own distorted perceptions." Play every epic note on Vai's 2012 release with these authentic transcriptions. Includes the title track and: Book of the Seven Seals • Creamsicle Sunset • Gravity Storm • John the Revelator • The Moon and I • Mullach a'tSi • No More Amsterdam • Racing the World • Sunshine Electric Raindrops • and more.

00110385 Guitar Recorded Versions...........$22.99

THE ULTRA ZONE

INCLUDES TAB On this album that the *All Music Guide* calls "an amazing exhibition of six-string talent," guitar virtuoso Steve Vai pays tribute to his mentor Frank Zappa on the song "Frank" and to Stevie Ray Vaughan on "Jibboom." This songbook also includes a special 8-page color section of photos and illustrations, and 11 more songs from the CD transcribed in notes & tab: Asian Sky • The Blood & Tears • Fever Dream • Here I Am • I'll Be Around • Lucky Charms • Oooo • The Silent Within • The Ultra Zone • and more.

00690392 Guitar Recorded Versions...........$19.95

INSTRUCTION

GUITAR WORLD PRESENTS STEVE VAI'S GUITAR WORKOUT

INCLUDES TAB Since its appearance in *Guitar World* in 1990, Vai's intensive guitar regimen has been the Holy Grail for serious players. Here is the lesson that shaped a generation of guitarists. Vai sat down with guitarist/transcriber Dave Whitehill and outlined his practice routine for the January 1990 issue of *Guitar World*. Never before had a guitarist given such an in-depth explanation of his musical exercise regimen. It became a must-have for guitarists. Many of the players interviewed in GW have cited it as an influence on their development as guitarists. Here's a chance to experience the workout in its original form and to learn some of the things Vai has done to develop his formidable chops and remarkable music vocabulary.

In this book, Steve Vai reveals his path to virtuoso enlightenment with two challenging guitar workouts – one 10-hour and one 30-hour – which include scale and chord exercises, ear training, sight-reading, music theory, and much more. These comprehensive workouts are reprinted by permission from *Guitar World* magazine.

00119643.......................................$14.99

STEVE VAI – GUITAR STYLES & TECHNIQUES

INCLUDES TAB

by Jeff Perrin
Signature Licks
Play along with the actual backing tracks from "Passion and Warfare" and "Sex & Religion," specially modified by Steve Vai himself! Learn the secrets behind a guitar virtuoso then play along like the pro himself. Songs: The Animal • Answers • For the Love of God • Rescue Me or Bury Me • The Riddle • Sex & Religion • Still My Bleeding Heart • Touching Tongues.

00673247 Book/CD Pack $22.95

ALIEN LOVE SECRETS: NAKED VAMPS

INCLUDES TAB

by Steve Vai and Wolf Marshall
Signature Licks
Learn the secrets behind this guitar virtuoso then play along like Vai himself with the actual backing tracks from *Alien Love Secrets*! Songs include: Bad Horsie • The Boy from Seattle • Die to Live • Juice • Tender Surrender • more.

00695223 Book/CD Pack $22.95

FIRE GARDEN: NAKED VAMPS

INCLUDES TAB

by Steve Vai and Wolf Marshall
Signature Licks
This unique package lets guitarists learn Steve Vai's style and techniques by playing along with the actual backing tracks from *Fire Garden*! Features 8 songs: Aching Hunger • Blowfish • Brother • The Crying Machine • Little Alligator • Taurus Bulba • There's a Fire in the House • Warm Regards.

00695166 Book/CD Pack $22.95

THE ULTRA ZONE: NAKED VAMPS

INCLUDES TAB

by Wolf Marshall
Signature Licks
Learn the secrets behind the signature sounds of this guitar virtuoso, and then play along with the *actual backing tracks* from *The Ultra Zone* – mixed and produced by Vai himself! In this unique book/CD pack, Wolf Marshall teaches you everything you need to know to play exactly like Steve. Songs include: The Blood & Tears • I'll Be Around • Jibboom • The Silent Within • The Ultra Zone • Voodoo Acid • Windows to the Soul.

00695684 Book/CD Pack $22.95

STEVE VAI – GUITAR PLAY-ALONG VOLUME 193

INCLUDES TAB The Guitar Play-Along Series will help you play your favorite songs quickly and easily! Just follow the tab, listen to the audio to hear how the guitar should sound, and then play along using the separate backing tracks. The melody and lyrics are also included in the book in case you want to sing, or to simply help you follow along. The audio is available online for download or streaming, and it is enhanced so you can adjust the recording to any tempo without changing pitch!

8 songs: The Attitude Song • The Crying Machine • Die to Live • For the Love of God • I Would Love To • Sunshine Electric Raindrops • Tender Surrender • Touching Tongues.

00156028 Book/Online Audio.....................$19.99

DVDs

ALIEN LOVE SECRETS

DVD Now on DVD, the full-length matching video to one of his albums. This video includes full performances of all seven songs from *Alien Love Secrets*. The performance features Steve's power trio of Robbie Harrington on bass, Chris Frazier on drums, and of course Steve himself on guitar. This unique performance video format allows you a special view into both Steve's guitar playing, as well as the creative musical mood and aura of each song. Featured songs include: Juice • Die to Live • and the grand finale power guitar ballad "Tender Surrender." 40 minutes.

00320540 DVD.................................$19.95

LIVE AT THE ASTORIA LONDON **DVD**

Favored Nations
Steve Vai, Billy Sheehan, Tony MacAlpine, Virgil Donati, Dave Weiner – Live in London! If you couldn't be at the Astoria for these extraordinary shows, then this DVD is the next best thing: an unbelievable concert video featuring backstage and behind-the-scenes footage, interviews, band biographies, a Vai discography, rehearsal coverage, and 21 songs – nearly 4 HOURS of footage! Also features Dolby Digital 5.1 Surround Sound, PCM Stereo, Audio Commentary, and Instant Chapter Access to Songs.

00320433 DVD.................................$19.95

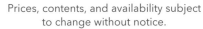

HAL•LEONARD®
www.halleonard.com

1118
028